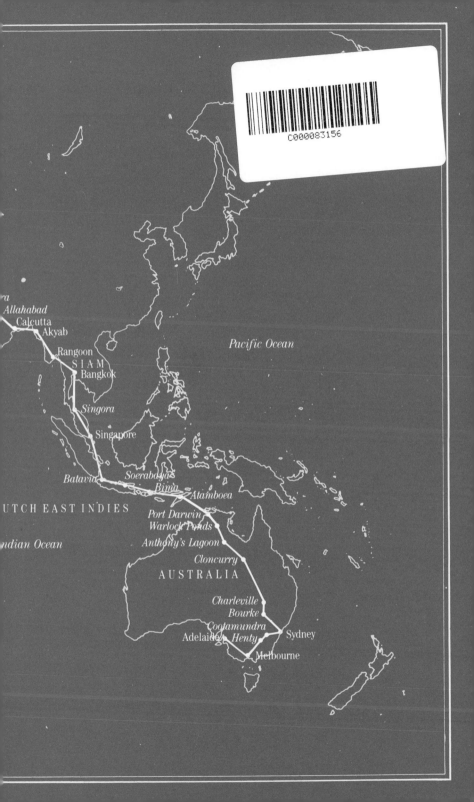

KANGAROO ROUTE

KANGAROO ROUTE

The development of commercial flight
between England and Australia

Meredith Hooper

ANGUS
& ROBERTSON
PUBLISHERS

*All distances in this book
are given in kilometres
with a conversion to statute miles;
altitude is in feet.*

ANGUS & ROBERTSON PUBLISHERS
London · Sydney · Melbourne

*First published in Australia by Angus & Robertson Publishers in 1985
First published in the United Kingdom
by Angus & Robertson (UK) Ltd in 1985*

Copyright © Meredith Hooper 1985

*National Library of Australia
Cataloguing-in-publication data.*

Hooper, Meredith.
Kangaroo route.

*Includes index.
ISBN 0 207 15086 9.*

*1. Aeronautics, Commercial – History.
2. Aeronautics – Flights – History.
I. Title.*

387.7

*Typeset in 12pt Bauer Bodoni by Graphicraft Typesetters
Printed in Singapore*

For
RICHARD

For
RICHARD

Contents

Foreword

It is easy to imagine that the urge to shorten communications between Australia and Great Britain would embroil many interesting characters. A few were able to foresee and expect that the aeroplane would become the solution to this almost insoluble problem. Others were like C. G. Grey, editor of the *Aeroplane*, who said in 1930 that aircraft would never progress beyond 40,000 lbs [18,160 kg] as, like the legs of the mammoth, the undercarriage would grow in weight as the square of the machine, and at 40,000 lbs the aircraft would have no payload. One prominent Australian politician of the time said that aircraft would never be able to fly to New Zealand from Australia.

Lord Wakefield, with few words, provided money for pioneering airmen and airwomen. The Shell Oil Co. provided prints of landing grounds all along the Kangaroo Route, even those in the most obscure locations. The Works Superintendent at Alor Star, in Malaya, laboured to get worried airmen off his mud patch and comforted them with a meal.

To include all those involved in the evolution of the Kangaroo Route would take several heavy tomes. This book for the first time tells in clear steps, remarkably free from side issues and speculation, a story that is a pleasure to read and I am honoured to be able to write this Foreword.

Captain G. U. Allan, CBE, AFC, AFR Ae S

Note on Sources

Much of the material on which *Kangaroo Route* is based was published in the 1920s and 1930s: accounts of their flights by aviators and passengers in books, magazines and journals; files of the *Aeroplane* and minutes of Royal Aeronautical Society meetings; house magazines of Qantas and oil companies; and Imperial Airways records. I have also used interviews recorded with Qantas captains of the 1930s made by the late David Jones; histories of commercial aviation, airline companies and airmail; and several modern biographies.

Acknowledgements

I would like to acknowledge help in research given by Arnold Nayler, Royal Aeronautical Society, London; Tony Harald, RAF Museum, Hendon; Jim Rankin, Barbara Thomas, Janice Ball and John White, Qantas; and Ronald Wilson, Historical Aviation Service, Ruislip.

Captain G. U. Allan and Mr E. A. Crome provided information, and photographs from their own collections.

Assistance in finding and providing pictures was given by Qantas; British Airways; KLM; Vickers; BAPCO, Bahrain; RAF Museum, Hendon; and the National Postal Museum, London.

I am very grateful.

Meredith Hooper
London

"The long, long trail to Australia of the pioneer, the racing airman or airwoman, the stunt artist, is today for the first time open to the ordinary man in the street."
—*Richard Coke, first through passenger from England to Australia, April 1935*

1
The Great Air Race

"YOU ARE FOOLS." The Vickers Aircraft managers stare at the Australian airmen.

"You boys have done all you were asked to do in the war. Now you are going to throw your lives away trying to fly to Australia."

Captain Ross Smith goes through the reasons again. The government of Australia has offered a very large prize for the first flight from England to Australia. It must be made by an Australian crew flying a British Empire-constructed aircraft and be completed within 720 consecutive hours (30 days). Other rules for competing are tight because accidents and disasters won't do the cause of aviation any good. Ross wants to enter the race with a twin-engined long-range bomber, the Vickers Vimy. It should be able to fly the necessary distance carrying a payload of petrol instead of bombs. And a Vimy has just proved its worth by flying across the Atlantic Ocean, the first-ever aircraft to make the journey non-stop, 16 hours 27 minutes in the air. John Alcock the pilot and Arthur Whitten Brown the navigator have won a small fortune in prize money. The England-to-Australia flight is the other great challenge of 1919—and worth the same money.

"Exactly," interrupt the Vickers people. They have gained the prestige of the Atlantic flight. Why risk a second Vimy on this harebrained, highly dangerous scheme to fly across the world? Look at the number of aircraft that crashed attempting the Atlantic.

But Ross Smith points out that he has actually flown over part of the route. He and his two aircraft mechanics, Jim Bennett and Wally Shiers, have just come back from the first-ever flight between Egypt and India. And they had the chance to travel on by sea from India as far as the islands of the Dutch East Indies (Indonesia), looking for places where an aeroplane could land.

Ross Smith's patron and friend, Brigadier-General "Biffy" Borton, pushes the young Australian's case hard with Vickers. Smith has had an outstanding war career as the ace pilot of No. 1 Squadron, Australian Flying Corps, in the Middle East. He is an extraordinarily courageous and skilful pilot, cool in danger, an efficient organiser, a charming and courteous man.

The Vickers company give in and show the airmen a spare Vimy in a hangar. Bennett and Shiers will sit in the rear gunner's cockpit sharing the space with as many spare parts as possible. Ross is pilot, his elder brother, Keith, navigator and back-up pilot. Extra fuel tanks are fitted. Ross watches the Vimy's weight carefully—the strain on the engines must be minimised. There is no weight spare to carry personal possessions, or one of the heavy new radios, but tins of bully beef and army biscuits are packed along with a fishing line in case they are forced down somewhere where they can use it.

Five aircraft are officially entered for the Great Air Race, the most momentous flight ever attempted. England to Australia is about the furthest distance

The Vickers Vimy crew in uniform, November 1919: (from left)
Sgt Wally Shiers, Lieut. Keith Smith, Capt. Ross Smith
and Sgt Jim Bennett (Vickers)

anyone can imagine taking an aeroplane. It is a grand,
crazy challenge. The top of the world to the bottom,
leaving Europe behind, flying across mountains, deserts, swamps and jungles, across tropical seas, over
the temples of the ancient world and the tents of
warring tribes, over the lands of the Egyptians, Arabs,
Jews, Turks, Persians, Indians, Burmese, Siamese,
Malays. The distance is seven times the journey across
the Atlantic, but there is one great advantage—it will
be possible to keep above solid ground much of the
way, and avoid long dangerous flights over the open
sea, except at the end. The route allows shortish hops
and frequent stops. Emergency landings are possible
when there is earth beneath.

Ross and Keith Smith, Jim Bennett and Wally
Shiers take off on Wednesday 12 November 1919
from the official starting aerodrome at Hounslow near
London in weather declared entirely unsuitable for
flying. The Great War ended 12 months and one day
ago. Now they are on their way home to see families
and friends, travelling by a method no-one has ever
before attempted. England to Australia by sea takes
just over five weeks. They plan to do it in four.

Snow and fog have come early this winter.
They battle through bitter conditions over France with
ice clotting on their goggles and snowstorms blocking
off all view of the world below. In Pisa, Italy, on the
fourth morning they almost fail to get the Vimy off the
rain-soaked mud-thick airfield. Ross Smith considers
this first section of the flight, London to Cairo, Egypt,
the most difficult. None of them has ever flown over
Europe. The weather is treacherous, the hours of
daylight brief. They risk being held up by snow or
unusable landing grounds. Down Italy, across to
Greece and out to the island of Crete the weather
continues foul with clouds and rain forcing them to fly

Snow covers the ground on the morning of 12 November 1919, just before the departure of the Vickers Vimy G-EAOU from Hounslow, near London (Vickers)

dangerously low. The four-hour flight over the Mediterranean to Africa is uneventful, but flying along the coast towards Cairo one engine runs hot. A pipe is cracked and there are no spares in Egypt, and none can be sent out from England for weeks. They try a repair with a gift of Wrigley's Spearmint chewing gum, well chewed, and it works. The Vickers Vimy has reached Cairo in a week, as planned, with skill, determination, teamwork and luck.

Only one other competitor in the race ever got beyond Europe, after being delayed for two months by drifting snow, floods, engine failure, petrol shortages and imprisonment as spies in Yugoslavia. Another aircraft, which left Hounslow the day after the Vimy, crashed within minutes of departing and both crew members were killed. One aircraft came down in the sea off Greece and both crew died. One aircraft turned back with engine failure half an hour over the Mediterranean on the way to Africa and crash-landed in Crete.

The Vickers Vimy leaves Cairo in bad weather and flies through miserably cold driving rain over the desert to Damascus, above sites of battles so recently fought. The next day the Smiths land at an army camp in the desert, short of Baghdad, because darkness is coming. They are woken in the night by a violent sandstorm which damages the Vimy's control wires. Then on to Basra at the head of the Persian Gulf, weary, keeping up a tight schedule of flying, maintenance, refuelling the Vimy's tanks by hand with, at times, over a tonne of petrol—10 to 16 hours' work every day before they can fall into bed, to be woken again at dawn. Down the wild remote northern side of the Persian Gulf, landing at the oasis of Bandar Abbas, then on, along the even more mountainous isolated coast to Karachi, in India. One day flying, one day resting, two days flying across the width of India to Calcutta. The end of the second section, and it has been the easiest, because Ross Smith has done it once before.

Taking off from the racecourse at Calcutta on the eighteenth day they avoid disaster from a bird strike by the greatest luck, fly on around the Burmese coast to Akyab, on to Rangoon, across treacherous unmapped cloud-covered mountains to the Siamese capital, Bangkok. South now through torrential monsoon storms with eyes in acute pain from pelting rain, to near disaster at a newly cleared airfield at Singora where some official has not realised that it is necessary, when removing trees, to take out the stumps as well. A sleepless night spent repairing the tail skid, then holding the Vimy down as the monsoon storm catches up with them. On after a day's delay to a hazardous landing on the racecourse at Singapore— far too small a space for the big machine. The third section of the journey is over. They are still eight days inside the 30 allowed, so they take a day to carry out essential maintenance on the Vimy.

No aircraft has ever had to sustain a continuous flight of this length. The last section ahead will involve flying in unknown weather conditions over a remote part of the world with only primitive and minimal landing grounds, except for the first night in Batavia (Jakarta) where there is a Dutch flying school. But first, heavy with fuel, the Vimy must make a perilous take-off from the Singapore racecourse. They get above houses and trees at a terrifyingly steep angle, the undercarriage scraping along branches, on the morning of Saturday 6 December, and head south. Batavia that night, then on down the island of Java to a specially prepared landing field at Surabaya, which turns out to be a deceptive crust of sun-baked mud

The Vickers Vimy preparing for take-off down the "matting road" in Surabaya, Java, on 8 December 1919 (Vickers)

over an oozing bog. The heavy Vimy breaks through the surface and sticks axle-deep in mud. They work in the broiling sun with the help of the local people, lugging the aeroplane free, again and again. Tyres puncture, the Vimy sinks back in, it all seems hopeless. So close to victory—yet they cannot get a footing for the heavy machine. Then late at night someone thinks of constructing a double roadway of woven bamboo mats supplied by the local people.

Next morning the Vimy lumbers down the artificial surface, slews off, punctures another tyre, but they work on, anchor the mats so the slipstream from the engines does not toss them around, and this time they get off. On down the islands, landing twice more at spaces hacked from the tropical forest until, at last, the great test is ahead. The Timor Sea. Seven hours of flying across the open ocean to the northernmost coast of Australia, from the last possible island to the barren edge of the great continent. They have an aircraft that has flown for nearly 18,000 kilometres (11,000 miles), and two hard-worked engines badly in need of a top overhaul. They build a raft then leave it behind. They tie a bottle of water, some food and a Very pistol to the tail, because the tail of an aircraft usually sinks last. An Australian warship is stationed halfway across the sea. And they make it, on Wednesday 10 December, flying into the newly constructed Fannie Bay aerodrome in Port Darwin with 52 hours to spare. Total flying time across the world from London to Darwin: 135 hours.

Australian Prime Minister Billy Hughes telegraphed the successful Ross Smith: "You have broken all the world's records and you have shown the world once more what manner of man the Australian is. You have ... proved that with relays of machines and men

Europe can be brought within 12 or 15 days of Australia."

In 1919 the Vickers Vimy was in the big league of world aircraft; the two Rolls-Royce engines packed 720 horsepower. Fully loaded, the Vimy weighed 5,900 kilograms (13,000 pounds)—the weight of a London bus. But the Vimy was a flying petrol container. The fuselage was a narrowing rectangular box of wood and canvas filled with fuel tanks one behind the other with the cockpits slotted in between. The power of the engines and the strength of the aircraft went into lifting the massive load of fuel.

The Vimy pioneered the England–Australia air route carrying petrol and oil, one pilot, one navigator, two mechanics, essential spare parts, emergency rations, minimal personal possessions—not even a change of clothing—and some letters and papers. There was absolutely no weight spare for anything else. The flight was its own payload: successfully achieving it was the only aim. The Vimy travelled at an average speed of 134 kilometres per hour (83 miles per hour), flying between four and nine hours a day, and making 23 overnight stops between Hounslow and Port Darwin.

It was to take another 15 years before people and things became the payload between England and Australia. Prime Minister Hughes's prediction of December 1919 came true for a commercial mail and passenger service in April 1935.

2
Civil Aviation Begins

A IR LAPS AND EDDIES AROUND US, defining the edge of everything on earth, an ocean that starts at our fingertips, at the blade of every grass stalk, at the curve of every pebble, and fills all space on and up until, less than the height of Mount Everest, it thins and becomes less available.

To travel within this ocean of air seemed the most wonderful and exhilarating achievement for early aviators, who took machines up off the surface of the earth and controlled them in the sky. To these first aviators the earth was a glue which stuck to your aeroplane until you were freed to explore the unknown waiting air. And the earth was home, and reaching it safely a great achievement, longed for, like harbour for the sailor.

Pilots were flying in the air, but their machines were closely tied to the earth. Engines were unreliable, fuel capacity very limited. Pilots only knew where they were going by looking over the edge and matching what they saw below with their knowledge of the landscape, or features on a printed map. They learnt to read the shape of the land, to recognise the layers of hills and direction of valleys, the outlines of lakes and

towns, the track of rivers and roads. All the time they
studied the land below looking for places to come
down in an emergency. The texture of that surface
mattered all the time, because engine failure meant
making an immediate attempt to land. An aeroplane
could come to earth on almost any reasonably level
smoothish place with enough space for stopping.
Beaches were ideal, or a racecourse, but a playing field
would do, or a road, or a large paddock. The time of
the year mattered, and whether rain had just fallen
making the ground thick or slippery. The hours of
daylight mattered because it was extremely difficult to
land in darkness. The number of hours an aeroplane
could sustain flight was brief. Pilots tried to avoid
water. Long-distance aviators, like migrating land
birds, sought the land bridges—the built-up portions
of the earth's surface—to fly over. Like the birds they
had to come down to refuel, and rest. And the nature
of the territory they landed on—the friendliness or
otherwise of the local inhabitants, the language
spoken, whether the water was drinkable, the insects,
the diseases, the food—all mattered.

Aeroplanes travelled through the air but they
could not get very far up into it. No aeroplane could fly
above the rain, the winds, the sandstorms and duststorms and snowstorms, the hail and sleet and lightning of the layer of air immediately above the earth's
surface. A modern passenger jet passes through that
layer, the first 10,000 feet or so of the atmosphere, in
10 minutes in a normal take-off. The jet may spend
longer in it while stacking outside a busy airport
waiting to land. Passengers might feel the quivering
bumps of disturbed air, sense the unease of seeing
nothing but grey swirling cloud vapour outside the
windows, briefly notice rain spattering the sides of the
aircraft. Everyone flew within that unpredictable sky,

amongst those layers of potential violence, before the introduction of the modern pressurised jet. Aircraft had a practical ceiling of 10,000 to 12,000 feet. Much commercial flying was done at low altitudes, between 1000 and 4000 feet. Passengers jolted and jerked in updraughts and hot-air turbulence, aeroplanes slid and bucked in strong winds. Pilots flew for much of the time unprotected in open cockpits. They felt the burning sun on their necks and wrists, the hail slicing into their faces, they suffered the almost intolerable pounding racket of engine noise in their ears. But they also gloried in the new beauty of clouds. They learnt that clouds could be banked up higher than anyone on earth had ever dreamt. They began to learn the way air could move near mountains, or unevenly over the heated-up surfaces of the land. They learnt to watch for the big birds soaring high on updraughts and how to catch the same air currents. They knew that temperature and height above sea-level affected an aircraft's ability to climb. They knew little about many important theoretical matters because these were not yet understood: for example, the load an aircraft could safely carry, or how the distribution of that load affected stability. But they did know that the ocean of air was filled with unexplained forces and mysteries. They flew using the strength of their bodies, their senses, their judgement, their experience—and their instinct.

Passenger aeroplanes today are removed from a close relationship with the earth. They travel in the upper atmosphere above most of the weather. Countries and oceans slide past underneath like a smooth slow-motion film. Aeroplanes come down out of the skies two or three times in a journey across the world. They have lost any intimacy with the part of the earth over which they are travelling, or the weather im-

mediately above that earth. But until pressurisation
was developed to seal passengers and crew into an
artificially controlled atmosphere, enabling aircraft to
operate in the higher reaches of the air, what the earth
and the air immediately above was like mattered
minute by minute to all who flew in the sky.

In the summer of 1909, on 5 July, a Frenchman,
Louis Blériot, pushed the 25-horsepower engine of his
Blériot-type XI the longest it had ever run, and
managed to get from the French coast to the English
coast, although he lost sight of both France and
England, had no idea where he was for 10 minutes,
and landed by stopping the engine and literally falling
down 20 metres (60 feet) to the ground. Blériot's flight
was the first successful aeroplane crossing of the
Channel, and the first time an aeroplane had flown
from one country to another over the sea.
    When Blériot made his flight there were
perhaps 100 aeroplanes in existence. But the war that
began in 1914 took the simple flying machine of
sportsmen, inventors and dedicated enthusiasts and
hammered and hothoused it into a technologically
advanced weapon of war, with boundaries of performance and reliability far beyond anything dreamed of
before the fighting began. Tens of thousands of aircraft were built, and thousands of men trained to be
pilots.
    At the end of the war in 1918 aviation was in a
great state of uncertainty. The war had created an
aviation industry, and built flying into lives of young,
trained, eager men. But would the aeroplane be used
in peacetime? Governments reduced their recently
created air forces to a minimum. Britain alone ended
the fighting with more than 22,500 aircraft on
strength. The numbers tumbled as machines were sold

or given away. Ten thousand were scrapped. Factories closed overnight, manufacturers went bankrupt as the mouth of war shut. Fighter planes came off the production line at one factory in north London straight onto a bonfire.

Could the aeroplane be used as a new means of public transport? Blériot had managed to lift just himself across the Channel in 1909. Now, 10 years later, there were aircraft well able to transport passengers and loads across the Channel. Important passengers, mail and cargo had been carried quite long distances during the final stages of the war, and now it was over, the RAF, for example, was continuing to carry mail and passengers into Europe. Australian Prime Minister Billy Hughes, as one of those passengers, was encouraged by his experiences to put forward the idea of the England-to-Australia Air Race.

A few men were eager to exploit the potential of this new method of transport by setting up commercial airline companies using wartime bombers converted to passenger use. But were the wood and fabric aeroplanes, and their engines, reliable enough to survive the demands of a regular month after month service? Pessimists pointed out that the wastage rate of aircraft had been very high during the fighting. No-one was sure of the stamina of the war machine.

Much more important, could the public be persuaded to make a journey, to travel from one place to another, through the sky? People had to be convinced that the wartime image of daring high-risk pilots was all over. The war had required men to fly with unthinking courage, to do battle in the sky, to live adrenalin-tense days pushing themselves and their machines to the edge. Some of these highly skilled, committed pilots with strings of kills to their credit and medals on their uniforms could not contemplate

the humdrum and the disciplines of commercial
flying. They had been trained to a different tempo:
"I'm no chauffeur. I'm no mailman, I'm a *flyer*."
Commercial aviation had to shed this image, fast.
Business would not grow out of risk and heroics.
Commercial pilots must be seen to be careful, responsible and safety-conscious. Flights must take
place at regular times in reliable aircraft. Perfectly
good ways of travelling already existed. Trains
(although not in war-devastated Germany) were
generally efficient, ships were reasonably comfortable
and well organised, the motorcar was coming on
nicely. Why travel in an aeroplane? It was new, clearly
dangerous, definitely expensive, and uncomfortable.

People were willing to have a go in an aeroplane, just one go, to say they had done it. Pilots keen
to keep flying and earn cash at the same time bought
war planes cheaply and hired themselves and their
machines out as a kind of funfair attraction. Fly in an
aeroplane! Experience the thrill, the sensation! Little
aeroplanes took off from beaches and fields all over
England, Europe, America and Australia, selling
"joy-rides"—a quick hop up into the sky, a turn
around the local town and back down to pick up the
next in the queue. In June and July 1919, 10,000
holiday-makers took off from the beach at Blackpool,
an English resort town, to ride in the sky, 15 minutes a
time. Four thousand visitors flew at an aviation
meeting in Amsterdam, Holland, in August.

Some pilots joined aerial circuses stunting
"death dives", wing-walking and mock dog-fights,
anything to thrill a paying audience; and the crowds,
gaping upwards, dreaded yet desired the accidents
inherent in the stunting.

Joy-riding and stunting belonged to the world
of entertainment. The world of commercial aviation

needed to have rules and regulations and organised facilities before it could get going. For some pilots any attempt to control flying was a bitterly resisted insult—government interference where it was least wanted. They felt betrayed by any of their old wartime mates who got involved in regulating aviation. Discussions about what controls were necessary went on within governments and internationally at the Paris peace talks. There were continuing problems about whether the airspace directly above a country belonged to that country, as the British had at first argued, or whether airspace was to be available to all. Was there to be "freedom of the air", giving pilots the right to fly where they wished, or should the principle of "sovereignty of the air"—the sky divided into nationally owned blocks, unseen national boundaries rising up from the ground—be clung to, to safeguard national interests and national defence?

An International Convention for the Regulation of Air Navigation was agreed to in Paris and signed by some governments. Signatories agreed to regularise their civil aviation, although some of the rules were taken straight from shipping regulations and had nothing to do with aircraft. Aeroplanes were required to slow down and proceed with caution in fog or rain. On a more practical level pilots now had to be licensed to fly aircraft commercially and be passed as medically fit. Ground engineers had to sit exams. Aircraft could only fly with a certificate of airworthiness. Governments had to decide which wartime aerodromes would be handed over to civilian use. Customs and immigration controls were needed for flights between countries.

Small companies in Britain, France and Germany began trying out the reality of scheduled commercial flying during 1919. Routes were short, mainly between cities, allowing a payload of passengers, mail and freight to be carried alongside the necessary petrol. The first passengers on the first regular scheduled international air service flew out of London and landed at Le Bourget airfield, Paris, on Monday 25 August 1919, just six weeks after the first aircraft had successfully flown across the Atlantic. The first day of the new air route was marred by rough weather although it was the middle of summer. No meteorological information was available for the use of pilots— you took off and found out. One return journey from Paris that first Monday was so bumpy that the passenger, a newspaper reporter, was sick without stopping into the only thing available, his bowler hat, which he was holding ready to be properly dressed on arrival in London.

The airline business was so small in the beginning everyone knew everyone else. The little companies operated with a few ex-war machines. A fighter plane or day bomber could carry one or two passengers sitting in the rear gunner's cockpit. The big night bombers were converted to passenger use with wicker chairs in the bomb bay and curtains and luggage racks. Passengers who did not want to be squashed stuffily inside could choose to perch out in the wind and weather in the gunner's cockpit forward of the pilot, but only after a lecture about safety—don't stand up, don't throw anything over the side. Leather flying coats, helmets and goggles were lent for passengers' use as part of the cost of the ticket. If the weather was really cold some companies provided thick blankets and hot water bottles. Aerodromes were muddy fields with wooden sheds. There was at first no radio communication between air and ground, and none between London and Paris.

The London-to-Paris route was reasonably

straightforward. Pilots flying for Handley Page Transport took off from the grass field between the railway line and the Handley Page factory in north London, and followed the number 16 bus route into Marble Arch in the centre of the city, by which time the heavily laden aircraft had usually managed to climb to the height of 500 feet—one and a half times the tower of Big Ben. Pilots then picked up the main railway line going south out of London and followed it to the coast. Emergency landing grounds were marked out in fields but there were not nearly enough. Bad weather or fuel shortage or engine trouble forced aircraft down over and over again—17 times on one particular London-to-Paris journey. Pilots tried to fly below the difficult English weather, hedge-hopping their way south, skimming over the Channel perhaps only 10 to 40 feet above the waves. Once in France pilots picked up the line of the railway and followed it into Paris. The London–Paris route was popular with English and French airline companies. Two and a half hours in the air compared well with all day, or all night, in a combination of train, boat and train. This was the kind of journey where aeroplanes could prove their commercial advantage.

Some pilots were only partial converts to the new commercial harness. One, a Captain Hope, notorious for his leopard-skin flying helmet, was given an experimental enclosed cockpit on his huge Handley Page 0/400 ex-bomber. He arrived in Paris after a bumpy flight from London. "I can't see, I can't hear, I can't feel, caged up in that thing," he roared and, finding an axe, smashed the cover away. But most of the pilots were only concerned to get wherever they were going and return again, quietly, quickly and safely. The few passengers who flew tended not to complain. If you were frightened you didn't do it.

The pioneer days of travelling in the gunner's cockpit of a converted bomber did not last long in England or Europe. Airlines vying for passengers on the intercity routes had to sell speed, and their customers tended to be busy businessmen, or wealthy people seeking novelty. The airlines had to attract these customers to survive, so facilities and services were up-graded as rapidly as possible. The comfort of a toilet, food and drink during the flight, padded chairs to sit on, curtains at the window and flowers on the tables helped to counteract the reality of flying as an uncomfortable, bumpy experience in unheated cabins with no sound-proofing. Some of the aircraft built to attract the right clientele had cabins which looked like small luxurious drawing rooms, or the relaxed smoking room of a London club, except no-one was allowed to smoke because it was too dangerous. Very few passenger airliners were ever built. The massive scale of wartime production completely disappeared. Aeroplanes were hand-built now according to demand and that demand was tiny.

European governments heavily subsidised their infant airlines, or ran them as nationalised companies. Various British companies struggled to make money with some government subsidy, but generally failed. In 1923, despite opposition from the Treasury, the British government decided to join existing airlines together into a single monopoly company supported by taxpayers' money and backed with separate financing. The problems of state ownership or private enterprise, monopoly or competition on routes and methods of subsidy started right at the beginning of civil aviation. The British government opted with the new company for a hybrid: private enterprise backed by state money and protected by monopoly. The new company had one provisional title, British Aircraft

Several Handley Page HP0/400s, the largest British long-range bombers in World War I, were converted for commercial use after the war (RAF Museum, Hendon)

Transport Service, until someone realised it spelt BATS. So it was called Imperial Airways and came into being on April Fools' Day 1924 with 19 pilots, rather fewer aircraft and a total seating capacity of 119. The company opened with a pilots' strike over rates of pay and flying hours.

The routes from London over the Channel into Europe were already established. But the new Imperial Airways had great schemes. The various parts of the Empire should be linked together by air, speeding up communications between Britain and her overseas possessions and interests. Long-haul air routes would, it was argued, be essential for defence and good for business. Other nations had the same ambitions. The French were beginning to fly into North Africa, and they planned routes to South America and right around to Saigon. The Germans were getting into Persia (Iran) and South America. Albert Plesman of KLM Dutch Airlines wanted to fly his machines through to the Dutch East Indies, to the capital Batavia. Most effort in the United States was concentrated on carrying mail, not people, but a wealthy young New Yorker, Juan Trippe, who founded the airline company that became Pan Am, was sending passenger aeroplanes down into Central and South America. India was the goal for the British. Establishing a route linking the Mother Country to the great subcontinent must take priority. Another route could branch off down Africa to the Cape, and the Indian route could eventually be extended through to Australia.

The tiny aviation companies were grasping at the idea of long-haul air routes while they were still fumbling with the organisation and aircraft for the shortest of hauls. But air routes were being sketched into the airspace of the world, small segments of great plans. Sections were developed, then slotted together bit by bit like a jigsaw. The two ends of what became the England-to-Australia route happened first: the flights carrying passengers from London into Europe; and a section of air route inside Australia.

3
A False
Finishing Tape

ANY AEROPLANE AIMING FOR AUSTRALIA had to come in at the top end; Australia was bottom-heavy. Towns and cities were concentrated along the southern curve of the continent, where the climate was kinder. Ships worked their way through the oceans to ports along this southern base line, from Fremantle around to Brisbane, obeying the reality of human occupation. But aeroplanes had to obey geography. Coming from wherever they had set out, aeroplanes, like birds, strained for the nearest landfall, and that was the wild empty north of the continent, a coastline of mudflats and mangroves, crocodiles and wild buffalo herds, enormous tides and wide brief rivers; a land with a rainless dry season and a humid, mosquito-ridden monsoonal wet. Aborigines lived here, as they always had. There were mission stations, and cattle stations, and settlements along the Overland Telegraph Line, that swathe cut through the scrub carrying the news of the world on a wire strung between wooden poles.

The only town of any size was Port Darwin, a tough town, strange and uninviting to visitors used to Australian or European cities. Darwin had pubs filled with cattle men and overlanders, mine owners, prospectors and poker players, and the hunters of buffalo, sandalwood, pearls and trepang. Darwin had a meatworks, a telegraph station and a gaol, with cricket matches in the dry season when a six went over the cliffs into the harbour, and Australian Rules football in the wet, the Wanderers versus the Vestey's meatworks boys. Residents in the old stone-built Victoria Hotel tried to outwit hungry white ants by balancing their suitcases on shiny metal cigarette tins. The only way to leave Darwin was by monthly boat around the coast, or overland driving along rough bushtracks, or via a hazardous journey south through the centre by train then camel.

Aeroplanes heading for Australia landed at Port Darwin. But it was a false finishing tape. A whole continent stretched between Darwin and the cities in the south. One marathon had been run—another lay ahead. Before an aeroplane could reach the southern cities the pilot would have to fly another four to six days, and the first part of the journey would be over an immensely lonely, largely unmapped territory, remote and wild.

The route south from Darwin was pioneered by the Smiths in the Vickers Vimy, and prepared by two young airmen, Lieutenant Hudson Fysh and Lieutenant Paul "Ginty" McGinness. Fysh and McGinness had flown together, observer and pilot, in the Australian Flying Corps with Ross Smith in Palestine. Coming back to Australia after the war they could find no work they wanted to do, like thousands of other returned servicemen. But Fysh and McGinness had been trained in the new skills of aviation; they had known the glamour and terror of aerial combat, the absolute thrill of handling an aeroplane. That was a difficult world to give up. They tried to compete in the

England–Australia Air Race but their chance dissolved when the wealthy backer who had promised them an aircraft died. Instead they got a job with the Defence Department surveying the northernmost part of an air route across Australia for any incoming Air Race pilots to follow. No aeroplane in the middle of 1919 had ever landed in Darwin, or flown between the cities of Melbourne and Adelaide, for example, let alone across Australia.

Fysh and McGinness arrived in the town of Longreach out in the western plains of Queensland on Wednesday 14 August 1919. They walked down the dusty streets of galvanised-iron houses where the herd of local goats stripped everything worth eating, even the washing off the clothes lines and the advertisements off fences. Fysh and McGinness were wearing their uniforms, and they created a sensation. Airmen were rarely glimpsed heroes, thought of as separate from the ordinary run of men.

In Longreach water was pumped up 1000 metres (3500 feet) from deep under the ground, hot and undrinkable. Fysh and McGinness were planning places where aircraft flying the same distance above ground could land, aircraft that had travelled all the way from England and might stop here, in outback Longreach, because it happened to be on a direct line between Port Darwin and Brisbane.

The two young airmen left Longreach for the north coast on 18 August in a Model T Ford loaded with spare parts, petrol and essential supplies. In England that August the first commercial air services were about to begin. Alcock and Brown, now Sir John and Sir Arthur, were being lionised for their flight across the Atlantic. Ross Smith was planning which route he would take to Australia for the Air Race if he could get hold of a suitable aircraft. In Australia a few aeroplanes had barnstormed around the towns taking amazed inhabitants up for a once-only joy-ride. There were no commercial air services at all.

Fysh and McGinness had an adventurous seven-week drive across 2180 kilometres (1350 miles) of country, some so wild and inaccessible no car had ever got through. Fysh stayed on in Darwin, organising the first two landing grounds. McGinness drove back along what was hoped would be an easier inland route choosing landing grounds and organising a stockpile of oil and petrol tins for refuelling. He got Aboriginal women to clear an aerodrome at Newcastle Waters on the Telegraph Line, in return for two bags of flour, 24 sticks of tobacco and some red fabric. Fysh chose a finishing post for the race in Darwin next to the Fannie Bay gaol, removing a banyan tree and levelling two large scrub turkeys' nests. Then he waited for the ace of his Flying Corps, Captain Ross Smith, to fly in over the Timor Sea. "When the aeroplanes arrive," wrote the editor of the local newspaper, "the landing ground at the Police Paddock is sure to be visited by a large number of people, who are warned of the great danger to themselves and also the aviator, by encroaching on the open space where the machines are expected to land. An aeroplane . . . propeller, revolving at a fearful pace, would cut a human body in two without the aviator feeling the jolt . . ." (Sir Hudson Fysh, *Qantas Rising*, Angus & Robertson Ltd, 1965, page 88)

When the little speck appeared in the sky on the afternoon of 10 December Hudson Fysh, like everyone else waiting at the landing ground, was deeply moved. He felt that this was probably the greatest flight in the history of aviation. Ross Smith had just turned 11 when the first controlled flight in a power-driven, heavier-than-air machine was

Hudson Fysh (right) welcomes Ross Smith to Darwin in
December 1919 (Qantas Collection)

achieved, 12 seconds on a North Carolina beach in
1903. Now he was just 27 and he had brought an
aeroplane across the world.

The Vimy did not use the first few landing
grounds so carefully laid down out of Darwin. The air
route had been planned to follow the Telegraph Line
south, then branch off via cattle stations across to the
little towns of western Queensland, allowing crews
overnight stops with bed, food and water, and access
to fuel supplies. But trouble with an engine forced
Smith to land the first day, four and a half hours from
Darwin, on a dried-up swamp crawling with flies. A
cracked port propeller blade forced him down the
second day beside a track leading to the police station
at Anthony Lagoon. The crew of the Vimy were
discovering two facts about flying over their home
land. Heated air rising from the desiccated baking
surface of the continent could cause rough turbulent
flying conditions with sudden lunges and jolting
bumps. All four men were violently airsick. And a
certain amount of inland Australia was a permanent
landing ground: flat, usually dry and uninhabited.

After the propeller cracked, the two Smiths,
Shiers and Bennett camped in the shade of the Vimy's
wings by a bore in the immense loneliness of the
outback. The heat was so great the triplex eyepieces of
their goggles melted. At night the Vimy creaked as the
temperature dropped, and the wooden aeroplane
cooled down from the blistering day temperatures.
The propeller was repaired by Bennett and Shiers with
great skill and ingenuity using splints of wood from a
packing case, galvanised iron cut into strips and a
broken beer bottle as a carpenter's plane.

Three days before Christmas the Vimy flew
into Longreach, and Ross and Keith Smith heard that
they had received knighthoods from King George V. It

could take days to get from Longreach to the next
town, and if the weather was bad no-one could get
through. Yet here just outside the town was an
aeroplane that had come from London, England. The
Vimy's flight had a dramatic impact on Australians.
No longer was their country dependent on ships and
the sea for contact with everywhere else.

But the strain of the flight was telling on the
Vimy's engines. Soon after taking off from Charleville
on Christmas Day there was a sudden explosion and
flames flashed along the fuselage. Major repairs had to
be carried out at a distant railway workshop and the
across-the-world aeroplane was stranded in a small
Queensland town for seven weeks. Hudson Fysh,
waiting in Darwin for any more crews in the Air Race
to arrive, watched shoots and suckers of spear grass
sprout all over the smooth hard surface of his carefully
prepared landing ground within days of the start of
the monsoon. Within weeks the grass was higher than
his head, and prisoners from the next-door gaol had to
cut a runway with all the scythes and sickles in
Darwin.

"When we have a regular air service between
England and Australia," Fysh told the local people,
"Darwin will automatically be the first port of call on
the great aerial highway." But Hudson Fysh was
learning several important lessons. One-off pioneer
flights could achieve their destination to a specially
prepared landing ground. But a regular air service
would need aircraft stamina and aerodrome maintenance.

The Model T Ford "Tin Lizzie" in which Hudson Fysh travelled with three companions when he left Darwin in May 1920 to rejoin Paul McGinness in Cloncurry, Queensland (Qantas Collection)

4
An Outback Air Service

SIXTEEN LITTLE COMPANIES registered flying businesses in Australia in 1920. One was set up by Hudson Fysh and Paul McGinness to fly between towns on part of the air route they had surveyed through central Queensland. They called their company the Queensland and Northern Territory Aerial Services Ltd—QANTAS. Fysh and McGinness saw the little towns each stuck at the far end of a railway line snaking inland from the coast. An aeroplane could link them together ironing out the slow distances, the loneliness and isolation. When the rains came the black soil of the area turned into heavy cloying mud trapping people's feet and vehicle wheels like flies on a flypaper. There was hardly a bridge in the whole area, and flooded rivers and creeks stopped all travelling. It was a country of huge distances with bad communications. Aeroplanes were like the birds, able to travel above the thick scrub, the difficult sandy patches, the awkward river crossings—over the long dry stages or the country impassable after rain. Aviation was an obvious solution to Australia's problem of sparsely spread population and inadequate transport.

Australia and aviation fitted each other, it was

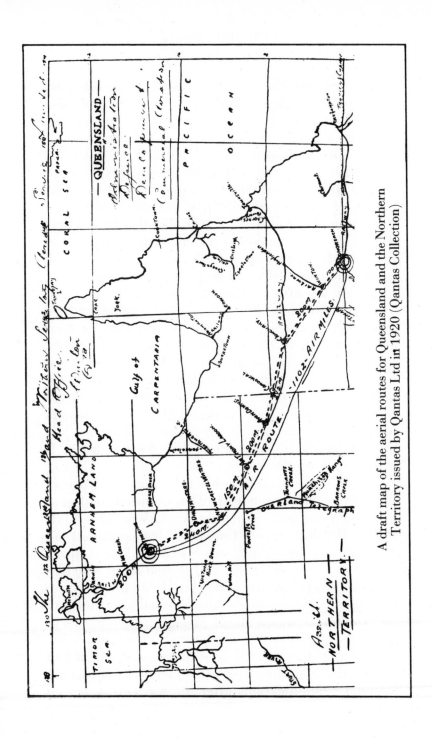

A draft map of the aerial routes for Queensland and the Northern Territory issued by Qantas Ltd in 1920 (Qantas Collection)

easy to see that. But the glove was far from ready for
the hand. Single-engined war-surplus aeroplanes
shipped out from England, often with no spare parts,
not even a repair manual, were not safe, not reliable
and horribly uncomfortable. Hudson Fysh described
the engines as cranky finicky things never to be
trusted. It took courage to commit one's body to the
passenger cockpit, in which two or three years pre-
viously an observer had sat scanning the ground over
enemy territory, anxiously watching the skies, gun at
the ready for enemy aircraft. Why leave familiar earth
for the dangerous sky in a recently invented machine?

All the little companies struggling to run commercial services in Australia lacked capital and resources. One crash could write off the bulk of their
equipment, their profits and unaccountable public
trust. Some of the companies employed half-weaned
war pilots who stunted with their machines, and the
many smashes and forced landings did not help the
cause of commercial aviation. Slap-happy repairs
turned machines into flying coffins. "Why not just
screw a handle to each side and be done with it?" It
wasn't such a joke.

McGinness and Fysh left Sydney for Queensland at the end of January 1921 with the entire fleet of
their new company—one First World War Avro 504K
with a 100-horsepower Sunbeam Dyak engine. Fysh
was piloting an army surplus BE2E for Charlie
Knight, a Longreach stock and station agent who had
bought the machine in Sydney but didn't know how to
fly. "Bloody Emergencies" the BEs had been called in
the war but it was a stable enough machine, except
that only 40 kilometres per hour (25 miles per hour)
separated its top speed from stalling speed, and it had
the usual minimal cockpit instruments. Fysh had got
his pilot's qualifications after the war ended, one of

the last batch of Australians to be trained in Egypt. He
had only 34 hours 50 minutes solo to his credit and he
had not flown since leaving the Middle East in March
1919.

The two aeroplanes ran into worsening weather
over hilly ground near Newcastle. Fysh dodged about
avoiding the clouds. It could take only seconds to
become disoriented flying blind in cloud, and Fysh
didn't have the experience to cope. He lost contact
with McGinness, then a large cloud bulked ahead.
What should he do: turn back? Barge on and hope the
cloud was thin? Stomach churning, nerves tightening,
frightened—but the decision had to be made, and
fast—Fysh tackled the outlying tendrils of the cloud.
Blank nothingness closed in. He concentrated on
airspeed indicator and compass, with steady pressure
on the rudder bar, the only methods of controlling
position in the air when all means of visual correction
by reference to a horizon had disappeared. But he lost
sense of the angle he was flying at and the compass
began to gyrate wildly. He had to get out of the misty
nothingness and into the light. Fysh throttled down
praying for clear air between the bottom of the cloud
and the top of the ground. The BE began the first turn
of a potentially fatal spin. Suddenly it came out into a
small clear patch of air in a valley with clouds all
around, a kind of hole in the greyness. The pit-head of
a coalmine, with slab buildings and sloping grey-green
bush-covered hillside showed to the right. Fysh put
the machine down and careered uphill dragging
through bushes, coming to a stop beside a cottage.

The BE had space for one passenger, and Fysh
was carrying Arthur Baird, their ex-squadron flight
sergeant who had agreed to join the company as
engineer. They were two out of three of the total staff
of Qantas and they were still alive. The miner's wife

came out of the cottage and offered them a cup of tea.

A wealthy Queensland pastoralist, Fergus McMaster, was backing the new Qantas company. McMaster felt obliged to travel as a passenger on the last leg of the journey to show his confidence. He had flown once before, a 10-minute joy-ride in England.

McMaster was waiting at Barcaldine, 105 kilometres (65 miles) from Longreach, and watched the two aeroplanes come in to land on a small claypan completely surrounded by gidyea stumps.

"The more you looked at that pan the smaller it seemed to get and the taller the stumps," said McMaster. He climbed into the cockpit of the Avro and McGinness swung the machine round in a cloud of dust and pebbles. "Like an athlete facing the high jump, he taxied back to over the edge of the pan into the stumps, swung round and opened the throttle, and if ever anyone realised that he was in the hands of God and the pilot, I did.

"Across the pan the machine rushed and cleared the gidyea stumps, and we were side-slipping and rocking in the air. Up and up we went, and then circled until Fysh got his BE off, and still we circled, climbing for height, and eventually we headed west for Longreach." (*Qantas Rising*, page 103)

A big summer storm was racing up with flashes of lightning and gusts of air which threw the aeroplanes on their beam ends, but they got to Longreach just ahead of it and landed to the cheers of the crowd. McMaster's only thought was relief at being back again on mother earth.

Next morning Charlie Knight, the stock and station agent, clambered up into the BE2E, one foot on the wing, one foot in the fuselage toehold and over the side, for a first flight in his newly acquired machine. McGinness was flying McMaster and another passenger in the Avro, and Fysh followed. But McGinness went in the wrong direction over ranges and heavily timbered country. The aircraft bumped and lurched in rough air conditions, and only just made it to Winton with a few minutes' fuel left. Charlie Knight was sick to the point of despair. He swore nothing would ever induce him to fly again and sold the BE2E to McGinness and Fysh.

Nine weeks later an Australian aviator, Bert Hinkler, flew his tiny Avro Baby aeroplane solo from Sydney up to his hometown of Bundaberg on the Queensland coast, 1130 kilometres (700 miles) in eight and three-quarter hours, establishing a world record distance for a non-stop flight in a light aircraft. Hinkler was an outstanding pilot who flew competitively in England. He had come to Australia by sea with the Avro crated in the hold, and he personally maintained and tuned its engine before the flight. Record-breaking flights like Hinkler's reached toward the limits of pilot and aeroplane endurance, and had little to do with the kind of flying McGinness and Fysh were trying to develop. They took 16 days on their rather longer journey to central Queensland, flying a total of $17\frac{1}{2}$ hours, at an average speed of 110 kilometres per hour (69 miles per hour).

A tin hangar on the edge of Longreach, two aeroplanes with a total carrying capacity of three passengers. The new company had to make money to survive. How? The first unofficial transporting of passengers had hardly been a success. The two aeroplanes were registered in accordance with the Air Navigation Act which had just become law, and Fysh and McGinness received pilot's licences. Then they took to the air selling joy-rides.

You could really only trawl an area once for joy-rides. Someone else had already flown through the

Hudson Fysh cleans the BE2E after a weekend of selling joy-rides at Thargomindah, Queensland, in 1921 (Qantas Collection)

larger Queensland towns creaming off the courageous. McGinness and Fysh split up and went out in different directions to the small outback settlements where almost no-one was likely to have seen an aeroplane. A telegram was sent in advance. Choose a clear level space free from stones, potholes and trees. Secure a white bed sheet in the centre so the pilot can see where to come down. Light a smoky fire to indicate wind direction. Leaflets advertised the coming event:

"The person who has not been in the air has not yet started to LIVE. Fly in the famous BE2E ... Have you ever had a flight in a British war machine?"

Almost the whole population would turn up and some brave souls would buy a ticket for 10 minutes' flying, capped and goggled and pushed up by the seat of their pants into the cockpit. As a bystander said, there was no need to wonder what ladies wore under their skirts any more. People seemed to feel the need to sign their names all over the fuselage and wings of the unfamiliar aeroplane, until it looked like some giant flying plaster cast.

Every night out on tour the aeroplane had to be guarded against souvenir hunters removing pieces, and animals chewing at the wing tips. Some old local could usually be found to act as night watchman, camping with his fire near the machine. Fysh and McGinness did not have to resort to the measures taken by a rival concern working a barnstorming circuit in New South Wales. A roll of barbed wire set up as an entanglement every night around their aeroplane did not prevent a bullock horning the rudder and ripping the fabric, or horses eating the wings. In the end cattle dogs were tied to this much-damaged aircraft, one to each wing tip and the third at the tail.

Race meetings brought good business. At Win-

dorah, on the Cooper, passengers crouched in the line
of a smoke fire to keep out of range of millions of
mosquitoes. The mosquitoes might be mocking humans' puny efforts to share the sky; but Fysh was too
hot and thirsty and bitten to contemplate anything but
the need to persuade another batch of locals to stop
watching the races and risk a flight, as the three-day
race meeting built up to a well-lubricated climax.
Even the dogs seemed determined not to be outdone
by their masters and were fighting in the streets, said
Fysh. He slept under the billiard table in the pub,
while thick smoke from a smouldering cow-dung
anti-mosquito fire added to the misery of the night.

Like other struggling commercial companies,
McGinness and Fysh took on any work they could get.
Joy-riding gave way to providing an aerial taxi service.
They flew stock agents between towns, the local
bookie, Possum Patterson, to race meetings, the doctor
to accidents at isolated homesteads. They dropped
boxes of chocolates by homemade parachute at the
homes of pretty girls. Anything to get people thinking
in terms of aeroplanes, anything to build up confidence in aviation. They managed to keep the company
going—just.

All the time Qantas was working towards persuading the Australian government to subsidise the
company by paying them to run an airmail service. A
mail contract was seen by the little commercial companies in Australia as the key to survival. The right to
carry mail and the government funding of the service
would underpin the setting up of a scheduled route,
with space on each aircraft for passengers and freight,
and the attraction of a regular timetable to lure the
payload. A subsidy had already been granted to
Western Australian Airways to run a long route between remote ports on the isolated western coast of the

continent. Two routes between capital cities were granted to another consortium. Persuading the Commonwealth government to support a Queensland route was a close-fought, hard battle. For Qantas it was a battle of survival. They could only continue in business if they achieved the subsidy. Fysh and McGinness flew between the towns on the proposed route cajoling people to lobby the government and put their money into the company. Qantas had to tender with sufficient and attractive aircraft to run the new service, and that took capital. Patriotism and national defence were rallying cries. Queenslanders had a right to the route, it was argued, and an efficient aeroplane service was vital to Australia's ability to defend herself. Aeroplanes would reduce the isolation of living in the outback, and encourage the hardy settlers.

Early in 1922 they got what they wanted. Qantas won a 12-month experimental government subsidy to run a scheduled mail and passenger service between the railhead towns of central Queensland, Charleville north-west to Cloncurry, with an overnight stop at Longreach where overhaul and maintenance work would be carried out. The distance of 920 kilometres (577 miles) on the map of Europe would have taken an aeroplane from London to the south of France.

Fysh and McGinness agreed to run the service with an untried stubby-shaped British aeroplane which looked good on paper, the Vickers Vulcan, known ungraciously as the Flying Pig. No Pigs being ready in time for the beginning of the service, two worn-out old Armstrong Whitworth war planes were bought as desperate substitutes. The Armstrong Whitworths overheated easily in the hot Queensland conditions and had to be coaxed up off the ground when fully loaded. They were "only just operable", said

Arrival at Longreach of the war-surplus Armstrong Whitworth FK8, piloted by Paul McGinness, on Qantas' first scheduled air service, 2 November 1922 (Qantas Collection)

Fysh. The tiny passenger cockpit was uncomfortable in the extreme.

McGinness flew the first 106 letters from Charleville up to Longreach on Thursday 2 November 1922. The service opened with speeches, cheers and much local excitement. Fysh was due to continue the second leg on to Cloncurry early in the morning of 3 November.

Waiting at the Longreach aerodrome in the quiet just before dawn was an 84-year-old man, Alexander Kennedy. Alexander Kennedy had been born in November 1837, a little after the newly invented steamtrain carried its first passengers. In 1878 he had pioneered a long dangerous trail by bullock wagon into country near Cloncurry. When Fysh and McGinness were begging people to back their idea of an airline company Kennedy put money in "on one condition", he said. "I am to be the first passenger when the service starts." And here he was, flying cap on, goggles waiting, last cup of tea in his hand.

Fysh had the old Armstrong Whitworth pushed hard back against the far fence. The wind was coming in warm little gusts. It was going to be a scorching day. The sky lightened every minute and he could see the crowd by the tin hangar watching his take-off.

Fysh opened the throttle and raced across the ground towards the distant fence. A moment of such pride. Queensland's first airmail flight from Longreach to Cloncurry and Qantas' first official passenger on the new service. The AW rocked as it careered across the uneven surface. *But it was not coming unstuck!* They were not getting enough lift! Short of the fence Fysh shut off and taxied back for another try. Followed by another. Back at the hangar, Arthur Baird ran up the engine and found that it was just down on revs, enough to make the difference. Hurriedly the other

Qantas passenger No. 1, Alexander Kennedy, aged 84, flew from
Longreach to Cloncurry on 3 November 1922
(Qantas Collection)

AW was wheeled out and made ready. Baird swung the propeller, flames jetted from the exhaust stubs. "Stay on the ground Mr Kennedy," urged worried friends. "Cancel the trip. It's too dangerous."

But the old man clambered up the fuselage, feeling for the foot niche and climbed into the cramped cockpit, mailbag on his feet. He had come up by train especially from Brisbane. He was not going to miss anything.

This time they made it. They were up and over the sleeping town, galvanised-iron roofs already glinting in the sunshine. Fysh looked around and saw the old man grinning happily, his flying cap slipped around his head, his white whiskers streaming in the wind. "Be damned," Kennedy shouted, above the noise of the engine. "Be damned to the doubters!"

Cloncurry was reached after two stops—498.7 kilometres (310.5 miles) in four and a half hours. Kennedy reckoned in the old days he would have just been unsaddling his horses and filling the billy at the waterhole 24 kilometres (15 miles) out of Longreach. What a revolution in transport.

On the return journey, Cloncurry to Charleville, Qantas carried Miss Ivy McLain, their first female passenger on the new service. She enjoyed, she said, drinking morning tea poured from a vacuum flask at 5000 feet.

Flying conditions along the Qantas route, as in much of Australia, were good: excellent visibility, clear weather and generally open country on which to make forced landings in reasonable safety. But the air of western Queensland, especially in summer, was hot and thin. The earlier a pilot took off in the day, the better. The cooler air at sunrise gave improved lift-off conditions for underpowered aircraft, and also more chance of avoiding the turbulent air that came with

The Vickers Vulcan, known by its critics as "The Flying Pig", was rejected by Qantas in 1923 (Vickers)

the heat in the middle of the day. Cunning pilots learnt to watch for thermals (ascending currents of air that rose over heated land) to help carry them upwards. The big birds of prey, like the Bromley kites and the eagles, were good indicators of the existence of the currents, riding them with outstretched wings.

The hot inland conditions doomed the Flying Pigs. A Vickers Vulcan sent out from England on a ship was unable to come anywhere near Qantas' specifications for climb rate with a full load (6000 feet in 13½ minutes). The Vulcan was an impressive monster typical of some of the commercial aircraft being developed in England. But it was a failure. Nothing like it had been seen in Australia. The stuffy cabin was beautifully upholstered with seating for eight passengers.

Qantas passengers continued to have to ride in the open cockpits of the ageing war planes which made up the company fleet. A sudden rainstorm could blow up with high winds and violent air currents, drenching them. In summer they broiled. When a duststorm travelled out of the central deserts every single thing was covered in fine grit. A thin layer of oil tended to cover everyone behind the engine in any case. Passengers were often airsick, into little cardboard boxes made by the men in the hangar and placed ready in the cockpit. In 1923 a secondhand Bristol fighter was added to the fleet, a fast powerful machine, like McGinness and Fysh had flown in the last stages of the war. The engine was lubricated by pure castor oil and the fumes added to the passengers' misery.

The 26-year-old McGinness left the company as soon as the regular service began: administration bored him. Running an airline was becoming a business of schedules, safety regulations, no drinking for pilots. He was a man of action—adventurous, extrovert—in many ways still the wartime pilot. Hudson Fysh, on the other hand, was finding the business of running an airline totally absorbing. He was a shy man, naturally cautious, introverted, with strong beliefs which he stuck to even if they made him unpopular. But Fysh was discovering that he had organisational skill, and a political sixth sense; he grasped the important truth that survival in civil aviation required understanding of worlds beyond piloting and machines. Fysh tried to keep to three safety rules: never fly in cloud (the ghastly experience out of Sydney in the BE2E remained with him), never fly after dark and always keep a line of retreat open in bad weather. He believed, obsessively, in safety. Commercial aviation would not survive unless passengers had confidence and that only came with reliable aircraft and an excellent safety record.

The Australian government insisted as one of the terms of granting a subsidy that Qantas employ an English pilot. Finding a suitable one wasn't that easy. The small-town atmosphere and primitive living conditions of Longreach sent many people back south to a more pleasant job. In dusty arid Longreach cooking was done on a wood stove in a galvanised-iron lean-to kitchen. No grass or plants could survive the bore water, vegetables came by rail from the coast, and entertainment was provided by moving-pictures twice a week in the open air. Flying the route, pilots had to get up before dawn, at 4 a.m., pick up the mail and any cargo, collect passengers from the local hotel if any were offering, and drive out in the company truck to the aerodrome where, in the pale dawn, cups of billy tea would be ready. Everyone helped push the aeroplane out of the hangar.

Some of the pilots who stuck out the conditions

for a while were what Fysh called true conscientious men, loyal to their aeroplanes. Some were independent-minded, eccentric men, wanderers, who soon moved on. There was Wigglesworth, who came with the Vickers Vulcan, and flew in bedroom slippers, and could drink any man under the table and walk out straight. And Vigers who liked chasing kangaroos, flying a bumping lurching route above the frightened mob at low altitude. He was very annoyed if he was expected to include passengers, and they proved his undoing. "I soon got bored flying up and down the Cloncurry–Longreach run," said Vigers, "and on one trip I was particularly bored and thought to myself, this old crate would loop; on looking around ... at the two elderly lady passengers and seeing that they were asleep, and I was so fed up, decided that I must have a little variation, and put the machine into a loop, but unfortunately the two ladies woke up at the top of the loop and looked what they thought was down and instead of seeing the ground, saw the sky and started to scream. It was reported and I was fired." (*Qantas Rising*, page 151)

Australia's new Civil Aviation Authority insisted on enough emergency landing strips along the route for an aircraft to be within gliding distance of one if the engine failed. Engine failure in a single-engined plane meant immediate landing. Spaces approximately 15 minutes' or so flying time apart were cleared and marked with a cross made of flattened petrol tins painted white. Forced landings on rough ground, while the machine careered over rabbit holes and tussocks of grass, frightened some passengers so badly they refused to fly again. The problem of bladder control meant many landings on a claypan, or by a dirt track, for a quick three minutes' stop, and relief. A forced landing with engine trouble meant the pilots and any passengers waiting until spare parts could be driven or flown out. The aircraft were maintained, or repaired after crashes, by the hard-worked ingenious engineers led by Arthur Baird, operating from the dirt-floored hangar at Longreach.

Qantas was a tiny shaky operation in outback Australia but it was surviving. Juggling its ageing and unsuitable aircraft around accidents and essential maintenance, it managed to run a scheduled passenger and airmail service while many companies in other parts of the world were failing. Its very existence had a far-reaching effect totally unknown to the men strug-gling to run the airline between outback Queensland towns. In London the Minister for Air, Sir Samuel Hoare, took encouragement from Qantas' example. Civil aviation in Britain was in a bad state. Reports of Qantas' achievements "were arriving in London at a most opportune moment. I urgently needed some striking example of practical air transport with which to persuade the government and the Treasury that there was much to be gained from civil air services." From the recommendations of Hoare and others that the separate English airline companies be merged into one properly subsidised company came Imperial Air-ways, in 1924.

In the first year of its service Qantas aeroplanes made 204 flights on the scheduled route, carried 156 passengers, 12,985 letters and 464 kilograms (1022 pounds) of freight. A total of 124,093 kilometres (77,108 miles) had been flown with no injury to crew or passenger, despite bumps and mishaps to aircraft. The little company had no guarantee of any future. "The general public have yet to be educated to the advantage of quick transit for themselves, mails and parcels," reported the Chairman in September 1923. But at the end of 1923 Qantas did get the vital subsidy

Hudson Fysh (pilot) signs for the mails while Qantas' first
engineer Arthur Baird (behind) looks on, early in 1923
(Qantas Collection)

renewed for one more year. And they had more aircraft—two war-surplus DH9Cs converted to passenger use: two people could sit in the gunner's compartment behind the pilot and one in front in what used to be the bomb rack for the Cooper bombs.

The year 1924 was the turning point: no crashes, the first profit, the first of the non-wartime RAAF-trained pilots recruited. The overnight stop at Longreach was cut out and plans to extend the route to Camooweal were approved. Taxi work increased. Qantas planes took on any work and carried everything—a pregnant woman to hospital, bottles of beer to thirsty shearers, mean cattle dogs with their drover masters, schoolchildren, the Prime Minister and his wife when rain blocked the roads on an official tour. Filled like a country bus, the little planes would heave into the air and travel across land where communications were slow and difficult, where a few hours' bumpy uncomfortable ride in the air could replace days of roundabout travel on the ground.

In October 1924 Qantas took delivery of an aircraft designed especially for passengers, the de Havilland DH50. A lid fitted down over the four-passenger cabin, so passengers did not have to wear cap and goggles. The single-engined DH50 cruised at over 130 kilometres per hour (80 miles per hour), and had a range of 604 kilometres (375 miles). The climb rate was acceptable: 5000 feet in nine minutes 48 seconds carrying four passengers and pilot plus luggage—a total of 527 kilograms (1162 pounds)—although this was far below the specified maximum weight. "At long last," said Hudson Fysh, "we felt we were on our way."

5

The Desert
Route

AFTER THE FIRST WORLD WAR the British were
given a chunk of the Middle East to control—
lands where great civilisations had flourished
and faded, where battles had been fought for
thousands of years, right up to the air battles of the
war that had just ended. Here were the countries of the
Old Testament and the New. Arabs faced Jews; Iraqis,
Persians, Syrians, Egyptians were uneasy neighbours.

East of Jerusalem as far as the Euphrates River
in Iraq was a desert which no European had ever
crossed in an east-west direction. An ancient caravan
route sliced across the desert from Baghdad to Damascus. But the desert itself was considered one of the
world's great barriers. Only the eagle and the vulture
flew across it. In 1921 the RAF were asked to organise
an air route from Cairo, across the desert, and on to
Baghdad: one-twenty-fourth of the way around the
world. The aircraft would carry letters, packages and
official passengers on a regular scheduled service,
establishing communications through the territory
controlled by the British. It was an all-year, all-
weather route which would provide valuable training
to the RAF. And once developed it would be a vital

backbone for the air highway planned from England to India, and beyond, to Australia.

The desert was a vast, unmapped, exposed, treeless plateau, mainly mud-coloured, sometimes striped with dull vegetation like a tiger skin, usually waterless except for wells dug in the rocks. Bedouin, belts stuck with knives and rifles, travelled from one water to the next with their flocks, camels and dark goat-hide tents. It was incredibly easy for the European to get lost in the desert. The eye would be fooled in the heat, and see things that were not there. The land repeated itself, yet was endlessly different.

Pilots needed to be able to look down and see a track to follow. If they force-landed near the track they could be found before they died of thirst. Officials thought about marking out a route by blasting craters in the ground every few kilometres with explosives. Instead, two exploring parties were sent during June 1921 in convoys of cars to survey a route. Their wheels pressed into the surface and the marks could be seen from the air. The winding twisting track made by the survey parties became the desert route. In places a tractor pulling a plough furrowed the line deeper into the earth. Emergency landing grounds were planned every 25 to 30 kilometres (15 to 20 miles). The tractor ploughed a large circle to mark the spot with a number or letter in the middle.

So the track was marked across the desert like a child draws with a stick in the sand, on and on. Winter rains washed away some of the marks, sections were straightened out and improved—the work of keeping the track visible never stopped. As the aircraft flew the route, RAF headquarters in Cairo and Baghdad were kept in radio contact and little flags slowly jerked across maps to show each pilot's position. Up in the air the pilots fought fatigue, the heat and glare of

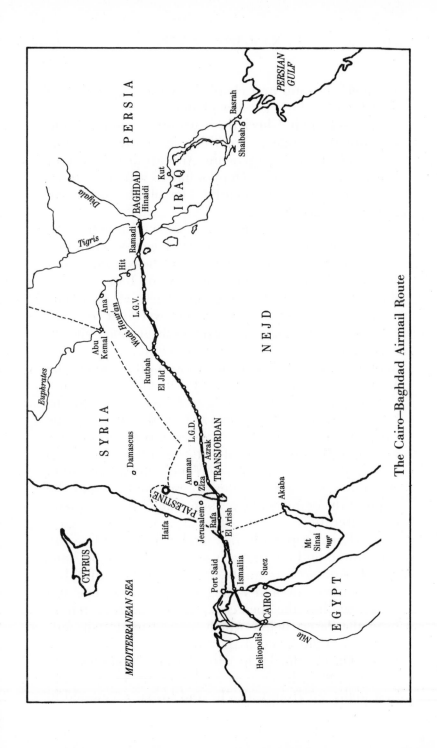

The Cairo–Baghdad Airmail Route

summer, the rain and clouds of winter, the strain of searching for the track down below. You couldn't take your eyes from it. Check the instruments, and the faint line would disappear. You'd lose it and have to start zigzagging to pick it up again. Aircraft flew in twos or threes for safety, yet each pilot had to watch the track and follow it independently. The blind must never lead the blind.

The RAF mostly flew Vickers Vernons—the famous Vickers Vimy with the fuselage thickened into a passenger cabin. The payload was heavy: mailbags, several official passengers, a crew of four and the desert equipment. The Vernons travelled as a self-contained maintenance depot and overnight bed and breakfast. The route was over high ground, blisteringly hot in summer, which reduced an aircraft's ability to take off. The payload was hard work and the Vernons rarely managed the 800-kilometre (500-mile) desert stage without needing to refuel. Petrol dumps had been set up at two places but the Bedouin stole the cans for water containers, so a steel box set in concrete was built. Bedouin fired rifles through the keyhole. So locked underground tanks were built and pilots had to remember to carry the key. Crews could spend the night at the empty railway station at Ziza, or camp by their aircraft.

Each trip with the mail was treated as an expedition, and anything, it was believed, could happen. The desert was empty, frightening, beautiful, but also monotonous and lulling to the senses. The sun beat down into the open cockpit; the heat reflected up from the desert below which seemed to stretch endlessly on. Men called it the "Blue".

On his third trip with the mail Roderick Hill had trouble with the port engine of his Vernon. The first night out from Cairo he and his crew camped in the desert working on the engine. Next morning they flew through hot disturbed air which caught the aircraft up then viciously dumped it down thousands of feet at a time. Hill's shoulders ached from battling with the controls. Suddenly a terrible vibration shook the aircraft followed by harsh banging sounds. The port engine was a wreck. Pieces of hot metal hurtled over the desert below. Bits hung off, wobbling stupidly. Hill managed to bring the Vernon down on one engine and landed near a great stone fort, built 2000 years before by the Romans. They were safe. The holed engine dripped hot dirty oil onto the stony ground. The desert wind soughed through the struts of the aircraft, otherwise there was utter silence. An hour later they had a telescopic wireless mast rigged up carrying an aerial to a small pole fixed on the aircraft. Hill cranked the handle of the generator to build up enough current, cranking it like a barrel organ till the sweat poured off him. Searle, the wireless operator, tapped out the message of distress. The Royal Mail was down. Help needed immediately. Hill watched as Searle moved the tuning knob and a faint high note came out of the air. Cairo acknowledging. Amman. Baghdad. Sitting there inside the grounded aircraft, so far from civilisation, the radio contact seemed a miracle. Hill felt close to breaking down, but the really hard work was ahead of them. It was no use being exhausted.

In the middle of the afternoon a second Vickers Vernon landed, picked up the mail and left—the mail must go on. The loneliness was worse after that. The great four-square fort of Kasr Kharana standing so grimly behind the grounded aircraft seemed filled with ghosts of the past. Hill was afraid to go and look at it by himself so he and a fellow officer went inside, through the square stone doorway, along a vaulted

The Vickers Vernon was used by the RAF on the desert route
(RAF Museum, Hendon)

passage to a central courtyard. There were skeletons in some of the partly ruined rooms with rags of clothing. One had been decapitated. The building had a peculiar eerie acrid smell which made them shiver.

The heat built up as the men waited under the shade of the aircraft's wings. Mostly the desert Bedouin were friendly but there were rumours of a marauding tribe in the area. The men had no rifles. Although they were out in the open they felt trapped.

At last, just before sundown, after many false alarms, three tiny columns of dust appeared away on the horizon, approaching very slowly but steadily across the level plain. The waiting men could see three dots, which turned into an armoured car with a gun turret and two vehicles equipped for desert travelling.

That night after supper cooked on a primus stove the men slept on the ground. The armoured car was parked facing outward, gun pointing into the darkness while sentries kept watch. Next day three aircraft flew in with spare parts. Everyone worked in the heat to replace the engine, working on into the darkness by the light of the armoured car's headlights. They went to bed dirty, sweating and thirsty, and were up at dawn on the third day to work on the engine again. Then at last, at 10 a.m., Hill could take off and complete the journey to Baghdad, arriving late at night, exhausted, sunscorched, unshaven—but safe.

Making the desert track and flying the desert route cost money, energy and some lives. The track was a frail thread but it was considered to be an important one. The desert lay across the route to India and would have to be conquered. The men who flew the route became affected by the experience. And, as Roderick Hill said, you got terribly fond of your aircraft. There it stood at the end of a long crossing, oil gently dripping off, stained by travel, engines silent after their great effort over the gaunt hills and vast silent spaces of the desert. For hours you had been sitting in the cockpit between the roaring engines, the wind singing through the canvas and taut wires. A journey that would have taken weeks of danger and difficulty by land had been completed in one or two days.

Sir Sefton Brancker, the Director of Civil Aviation, decided he must travel to India to discuss the proposals for an air route between Britain and her most important colony. He had booked his sea passage when he was persuaded to fly by a young pilot named Alan Cobham. Cobham raised the money to buy a DH50 with a cabin for Brancker by appealing to industrialists' patriotism. What a good advertisement it would be for British aviation if the Director of Civil Aviation actually flew to India, and back!

The political implications of wanting long-haul air routes were gradually being grasped, and Brancker needed to discuss them with officials in the relevant countries. It was possible in theory to fly thousands of kilometres inside Australia, the United States and Russia, and remain over your own territory. But everywhere the British planned to fly involved crossing foreign territory. Just across the Channel waited a complex of nations who considered the airspace above them theirs to dispose of, or refuse entry to, as they wished. Commercial aeroplanes had to come down often to refuel, and could not easily fly in the dark. That meant agreements had to be made with foreign governments for the rights to refuel, organisation of maintenance facilities and provision of overnight accommodation. Radio stations needed to be built and manned along any route planned.

The British were lucky with a good part of their desired route to India. Once Europe was out of the

Pilot Alan Cobham with the British Director of Civil Aviation, Sir
Sefton Brancker (RAF Museum, Hendon)

way, Cairo through to Basra at the top of the Persian
Gulf was within an area of British influence. Persia
must be negotiated with. Then the huge expanse of
India lay ahead, stretching from Karachi to Calcutta.
Beyond was Burma, the Malayan Peninsula, Singapore—all within British control—until the islands of
the Dutch East Indies. The map of the world would
change mightily in the next years—new countries, new
names, altered national boundaries—but in the 1920s
the routes through to India, on to Australia and down
to South Africa, were generally Empire-red.

Experts were deeply divided about the best
method of moving letters and humans long distances
through the air. Aeroplanes could only carry a smallish
payload fairly short distances, and even then engines
were unreliable, as the Vickers Vernons were proving
in the Middle East. On European routes Imperial
Airways were experiencing a forced landing on seven
per cent of all flights. Commercial air services needed
an elaborate, expensive infrastructure. They needed a
fleet of aeroplanes to keep a scheduled service going,
permanent fuel supplies, maintenance facilities and
meteorological information. Aeroplanes needed all-
weather aerodromes and ground engineers. Letters
were an uncomplaining payload: mailbags could be
stacked in the cold or the sun, shoved into any
available space, thrown from an aircraft if necessary.
But people as the payload had to have toilets, meals,
baggage handlers, airport reception facilities, ticketing
procedures. On a long-haul route passengers could
create horribly difficult problems. What could you do
with passengers during a forced landing in some wild
or desert place? Where would they sleep during
overnight stops? What would they eat? What would
happen if a passenger fell ill? How could they manage
different currency systems each day? Would they

insist on sightseeing? Would they mind getting up before dawn?

Many experts were arguing that airships were the answer to long-haul travel. An airship was the only flying machine capable of carrying a large number of fare-paying passengers plus crew plus a heavy load of fuel non-stop over a long distance, although at a slow cumbrous pace. Passengers could be serviced on board in some luxury in the roomy cabins below the giant gas-filled bag. Airships would be the ocean liners of the long-haul air routes. The arguments were very persuasive.

German airships designed by Count von Zeppelin had carried large numbers of passengers on successful cruises before the First World War. An experimental British airship, R34, had crossed the Atlantic both ways in July 1919, while those on board listened to gramophone music sitting in comfortable lounge chairs. At the same time Alcock and Brown struggled one way across the Atlantic in the open cockpit of the Vickers Vimy, frozen, cramped, semi-deafened and hungry. Now the Germans were planning bigger better airships for transoceanic travel like the *Graf Zeppelin*, at 236 metres (774 feet) the same size as the biggest ocean liner. The British government decided in 1924 shortly after founding Imperial Airways that two large civil airships should be built for the Empire routes: R101 funded by government money, and R100 funded by Vickers, representing private enterprise. One hundred passengers, it was claimed, would be able to travel to India at once, with their luggage plus 10 tonnes of mail.

On his arrival in India at the end of December 1924 Sir Sefton Brancker began arrangements for the building of an airship base in Karachi. A vast hangar and a mooring tower would be needed. But the two

British airships were only just on the drawing
boards—a service of some sort must begin using what
was available. Arriving back in England in March
1925 in Cobham's DH50 Sir Sefton recommended
that Imperial Airways make a start on the England to
India route by taking over the RAF desert service. The
well-pioneered Cairo to Baghdad route was handed
over by the RAF at the end of 1926: a ready-made
piece of the jigsaw.

6

A Return Flight

ALAN COBHAM WAS AN OUT-AND-BACK-AGAIN PILOT, the first British long-distance aviator who worked in terms of leaving for a destination and returning, all in one journey, and in the same aircraft. In 1926 he decided to fly to and from Australia in his de Havilland DH50. He had already flown it from London to India and on to Rangoon, and return, and London to Cape Town and back. For that hot high African journey he had equipped the DH50 with a new powerful 385-horsepower Armstrong Siddeley Jaguar radial engine.

Some experts who did not accept the arguments for airships believed that the flying boat or seaplane was the safest and most practical means of covering long distances, given the amount of water in the world and the lack of aerodromes. The problem of sufficient payload would be overcome as more powerful engines were developed. If all water could be home the difficulties of taking off and landing on inadequate or dangerous aerodrome surfaces disappeared. In an emergency surely it was better to come down on water, than risk the earth?

Cobham decided to make the point by converting his DH50 to a seaplane for the round trip to Australia. A pair of Short's duralumin all-metal floats were fitted and Cobham left England on 30 June 1926 with his engineer, Arthur Elliott, in the passenger cabin. A mascot, a small oak boomerang inscribed "I go to return", was carried in the cockpit.

At first Cobham thought how pleasant it was to take off without having to worry about trees and fences, a muddy surface, whether there were unseen telegraph lines to clear or whether a tyre might burst. But as the flight continued, landing and taking off from the various harbours and rivers turned out to be a difficult manoeuvre. Once landed on water with the engine shut off the little seaplane was powerless and could quickly drift with wind or current against rocks, boats, buoys—any obstruction. To Cobham, usually tired and anxious after long hours in the air, anything seemed capable of damaging his frail craft. The floats were only thin shells of metal. The fabric wings were so easily hurt. Landing in water meant relying on whoever happened to be around at that moment to help with controlling the aircraft and moving it to a mooring place. To his annoyance Cobham found that many people did not understand English. Over and over again he would be standing on one of the floats after bringing the machine down into the water, shouting instructions, bellowing threats, swearing and cursing, while local inhabitants stood by failing to comprehend what was required of them.

At the end of the first week, already very tired and strangely dispirited, Cobham was caught in a violent sandstorm as he flew over swampy country near the head of the Persian Gulf. He took the DH50 down very low, skimming over the reeds and water as he tried to see his way ahead. Suddenly a violent explosion seemed to come from the cabin. Cobham

Alan Cobham and his DH50, fitted with floats, in Baghdad en route to Australia, 1926 (RAF Museum, Hendon)

shouted through the window connecting cockpit to
cabin asking Arthur Elliott what had happened, but
he couldn't hear the reply over the engine noise. So
Elliott scribbled a note and handed it through. "A
petrol pipe has burst. I am bleeding a pot of blood."
Cobham flew doggedly and grimly on to come down in
the river at Basra, and cajoled then bullied the natives
to help lift the injured man out of the plane. That
night Elliott died in hospital. A bullet shot by an Arab
against the intruding plane had killed him. Sick at
heart and shocked by the loss of his friend, Cobham
only carried on when an Air Force mechanic called
Sergeant Ward, who knew a little about the DH50's
Siddeley Jaguar engine, agreed to join the flight.

The heat really affected Cobham and made
him feel exhausted. He reckoned it was one of the
greatest problems rising out of this new ability of
humans to fly across the world. How could anyone
cope with sudden changes of temperature? You could
leave England on a cool spring day and be in the
Persian Gulf four days later in stifling heat. This
would be difficult enough for fit people to manage. It
might kill the weak, Cobham thought. The other
problem was rain. The monsoon season dumped vast
quantities of rain over a wide band of the world, with
storms, lightning and strong winds. How could any
kind of regular air service be organised during the
monsoon? The difficulties of flying a small plane in
this kind of weather were immense.

Approaching Rangoon in Burma, Cobham flew
into such intense rain he had to turn away and try to
find another route around the cloudburst. More storms
loomed ahead. Cobham, seeing a steamer on a river
below, brought the seaplane down, shouting out for
assistance as his fragile machine began drifting help-
lessly into the bank. Amazed Burmese stared from the

steamer. They seemed not to comprehend his need for a rope to secure him to the steamer's side. They failed to realise, never having seen one before, that a seaplane, once the engine is shut off, has as much control as a paper bag on the water. Cobham thought a European must be in charge of the steamer. When he finally got aboard, in the pouring rain, he found no European, and no-one speaking or understanding English. "Where are we?" Cobham asked, jabbing at the map of the region he had brought aboard. It was obvious no-one had seen a map.

Cobham finally worked out that Rangoon must be to the north. Now he had to get up out of the river, a tricky problem with a wet engine. His little aeroplane was balancing on its floats and attached by rope to a steamer in the middle of a fast-flowing mud-coloured Burmese river, with thick jungle crowding down both banks and rain pouring in grey sheets, and nobody was available who could speak English. The engine must work! Luckily it fired first time. Cobham built up the revs, Ward chopped through the rope with an axe and they were off, shot like a stone from a catapult. The people on the steamer stared after them, the chopped end of the rope trailing in the water.

Crossing the Timor Sea turned out to be a long nerve-racking flight. The petrol was getting low and Cobham worried that he might have navigated incorrectly and missed Australia. After over six hours in the air, flying most of the time 50 to 100 feet above the sea, he saw land. Lonely and desolate looking, but it didn't matter, it was land. Cobham reached Darwin on 5 August, 37 days from London. The floats were removed and he flew the DH50 as a landplane on into Australia, down the Overland Telegraph Line as the Smiths had done six and a half years before in the Vimy.

Stopovers on a journey across the world were always varied. Unlike Ross and Keith Smith, Cobham had packed his dinner jacket and several shirts so he could be correctly dressed when entertained by governors, consuls and generals en route. On his first night's stop in Australia after Darwin, a dinner jacket was not necessary. Cobham found navigating over the vast featureless stretches of northern Australia very difficult. It all looked the same and there were no accurate maps to help. He thought he would be able to see the Overland Telegraph poles from the air but they were too thin. You had to look for a swathe of cut trees where the Line passed through scrub; or car or cattle tracks, faintly pressed into the ground—but then you had to follow the right ones.

With all these difficulties Cobham decided after hours in the air to land at Newcastle Waters, a telegraph station on the Line, and spend the night there. A policeman, and what Cobham called the "local postmaster", turned up in battered old cars. Cobham asked if they could spend the night here. "Aye," said the postmaster. "May we beg a lift in your car?" The postmaster didn't answer, just jerked his head in the direction of a car. They arrived at what Cobham described as a hut made of wood with chicken-wire walls and a galvanised-iron roof. Inside was a long table covered in linoleum, with six tin plates and three large Tate sugar boxes turned upside down. Three or four men came in and sat down in silence. The cook, a big fellow in singlet and slacks, sat down at one end of the table, the postmaster at the other. The three sugar boxes were lifted up—underneath was dinner. The flies raced in to the unprotected food. The men raced the food into their mouths. No-one said anything. Dinner over, the men left. Cobham and Ward huddled under blankets in the coldness of the desert night. Next morning the flies came out with the sun, and Cobham took off, leaving the Telegraph Line and branching east on the route pioneered by the Smiths to link up with the Qantas route through Camooweal and Longreach, coming in so low people thought his aeroplane was a motorcar. Australia is one vast aerodrome, Cobham wrote. You just land anywhere. It's ideal flying country.

Cobham received an enormous welcome in Sydney. Seeing a famous aeroplane which had actually flown all the way from London was incredibly exciting and overenthusiastic crowds broke down the barriers. Melbourne produced a near riot as thousands of people pushed aside the barriers and rushed onto the landing ground, then trampled the official enclosure and temporary broadcasting station. People were crushed in the crowd. By what seemed a miracle, nobody was mangled by the whirling propeller. Cobham was carried by police into a hangar just ahead of the crowd, then locked into a corrugated-iron room. Boys clambered up the walls outside and jumped on the roof.

Cobham left Adelaide on 30 August and flew north. Stopping to refuel at Newcastle Waters, he and Ward dropped off a large ham for their silent hosts of three weeks before. Supplies for the telegraph station came up once a year from Adelaide by camel. An air-lifted ham was a remarkable addition to the local diet. Aeroplanes could not help but be useful in Australia, Cobham noted.

The monsoon storms in Malaya and Burma were so heavy that Cobham was delayed over and over again. "No regular air service to Australia can exist," he reported, "until radio communication is established between landing places, and weather-forecasting services are set up."

The DH50 made a dramatic landing on the River Thames in front of the Houses of Parliament on the first day of October 1926. The round trip to Australia—the first ever—had been completed in three months. A ship could do it faster, but Cobham had travelled in a small aeroplane. Enthusiastic crowds welcomed the airmen home, and Cobham became another knight of the air—Sir Alan.

7
A Grand Tour

"THIS IS NOT A MILITARY FLIGHT. A woman is therefore not contraband. I intend to take my wife, Lady Maude."

Sir Samuel Hoare, Secretary of State for Air, decided to inaugurate Imperial Airways' long-haul air route from England to India by travelling on it himself with his wife. The propaganda value would be enormous. Sir Samuel was determined to prove that the aeroplane was a reliable, humdrum, unsensational means of transport, and a real asset to the British Empire. Unfortunately the only time that suited him to travel was after Christmas, during the parliamentary holidays, which meant flying during the risky European winter weather. No member of the British Cabinet had ever contemplated a long journey by air. Worried friends tried to dissuade the Hoares but they ignored all warnings of danger. The Prime Minister was annoyed. One member of his Cabinet was diving in Madeira, one skiing in the Alps and now Sam Hoare intended flying to India. "I feel like a circus manager whose performing fleas have escaped." "Scarcely anyone was taking aviation seriously," said Hoare sadly.

Sir Alan Cobham's recently completed flight to
Australia and back had aroused enormous public
interest, but it was a one-off event. Commercial air
services over a long-haul route were an entirely different matter, as Hoare knew. Flights with the mails
and passengers had to be regular, to schedule, and they
had to be seen to be safe. Lady Maude intended to
prove to a doubting public that flying long distances
was not an adventure for men only. It could be a
normal and dependable method for everyone—or
certainly at least for Cabinet Ministers' wives.

Lady Maude spent some time on the problem of
her clothes; no female had ever flown to India. One
well-known woman pilot begged to come as her maid,
just to experience the flight. She offered to help with
piloting the aircraft, but all the places were taken by
officials. Lady Maude had to work out how, after
hours in the aeroplane, to arrive smartly dressed to
attend an official function, without the help of a maid
and with the minimum weight of luggage. Lightweight
luggage had not been invented and she was allowed to
take only one suitcase and one dressing case. Lightweight containers for necessities like face powder and
bath salts did not exist either and Lady Maude used
great ingenuity in finding aluminium containers, like
picnic butter tins, to replace breakable china and
glass. Of course all the heavy luggage for activities in
India went on ahead by sea. But during the flight she
had to be prepared for sun and rain, heat and cold,
deserts and drawing rooms. The most useful articles of
clothing turned out to be gumboots for wet aerodromes, and a dressing-gown which could be worn
on the plane. She chose two basic outfits: a woollen
jumper and tweed skirt, and a coat and skirt in the
new stockinette material, worn with a crepe de Chine
jumper. Then she added layers of woollen coat, leather

coat, fur coat, according to the temperature, and of course a felt hat. And she packed a black lace evening dress for dining with emirs and kings along the way.

Imperial Airways had asked the de Havilland company to design a strong reliable aircraft for the new Cairo to Karachi route. Given the inhospitable terrain, forced landings must be kept to a minimum, so three engines were specified. De Havilland produced the DH66 Hercules, a biplane of the usual wood and fabric construction, with an open cockpit for pilot and navigator, a divided cabin with room for the engineer and wireless operator in the forward part and 14 passengers in the rear section. Only seven seats were fitted because the weight of mailbags reduced the number of passengers that could be carried safely. The new aircraft had an endurance of five hours in the air. Imperial Airways ordered a fleet of five Hercules (the name was chosen in a competition run by *Meccano Magazine*).

A rather anxious crowd gathered at Croydon Airport outside London well before dawn on Boxing Day 1926. The aircraft for the inaugural flight had only just been built in time. Engines were being tested all through Christmas Day, and there was no opportunity for a trial long-distance flight. Sir Samuel and Lady Maude walked across the frosty grass towards the aeroplane which was to be their home for the next 11 to 12 days. The photographer's flashlight revealed the bulk of the machine, the pale faces of the little procession, then all was dark again. Inside the cabin they could just make out the seats. Then they were off. They had drawn up their wills. They had the latest life-saving waistcoats for crossing the Mediterranean, which was considered to be a very dangerous thing to do in a landplane.

The weather worked into a raging gale with

sleet slamming against the windows. The aircraft felt like an express lift constantly starting at the top of the tallest building and descending, fast, to the bottom then repeating the process again and again. The passengers huddled in their seats, miserably cold and almost all airsick. After four hours the DH66 landed at the military aerodrome at Dijon in France for the first of the official visits. Sir Samuel and Lady Maude lurched out to be greeted by military and civic dignitaries, bands, speeches, bouquets of roses and, most difficult under the circumstances, boxes of chocolates. The French military aircraft sent up as an escort had been unable to locate the DH66 in the clouds and sleet.

Each day's journey was divided into two stages of about 480 kilometres (300 miles). Every day the captain landed at lunchtime to refuel the machine, and his passengers. Much publicity surrounded the journey. Everywhere they came down the official welcomes, speeches and banquets were repeated. After a week they reached the brown-coloured city of Baghdad, narrow streets and mosques between the dark green of palm groves. At Baghdad the Hoares dined with King Feisal and discussed the new air route with the Iraqi government. Next morning they flew over the seemingly unending reedy marshes where the Tigris and Euphrates meet. Cobham's mechanic Elliott had been shot at and killed here only a few months before. They arrived at Basra, close to the frontier between Iraq and Persia, for lunch. Here they left the security of the air route pioneered by the RAF which they had been following from Cairo across the desert track to Baghdad and down to this port at the top of the Persian Gulf. Ahead was desolate wild country. Few people travelled between the Persian Gulf and the north-west frontier of India. Here seven

Imperial Airways' DH66 Hercules, *City of Cairo*, being refuelled on the Cairo–Karachi route (RAF Museum, Hendon)

years ago Ross and Keith Smith had carried a docu-
ment begging kind treatment in case of a forced
landing. Sir Samuel carried a letter pointing out that
he was an exalted person proceeding with his wife,
staff and servants on an urgent and important mission
for Britain, and that his safety was a matter of the
closest concern to the King of England.

The first night was spent at Bushire, an oasis
jutting out into the Persian Gulf. At all stops people
came to stare at the aeroplane. There were black-
coated representatives of the Persian government, and
women with faces covered by skull-like masks. At one
stop a Persian official sat at a wooden table in the
desert to process their passports. The country was
either arid desert or high, jagged, weirdly shaped
mountains. Sir Samuel thought it all looked diabolical
and hideous. There appeared to be almost nowhere for
emergency landings.

They reached Jask on the second afternoon
from Basra, and found they could only get to the
telegraph station, where they were to sleep the night,
by camel. Jogging uncomfortably along, the Hoares
listened to the tales of local life told by the manager,
Mr Janes. It rained two centimetres (three-quarters of
an inch) a year at Jask. The flies died of heat in the
summer. The telegraph messages at the station were
punched out on paper tape and the local cows were so
hungry that they ate the tape. The Hoares heard
stories of this desolate coast—of slavery and pearl
diving, of pirates and dead men.

Next morning at 6 a.m. the Hoares set out by
camel for the aircraft. They were only one day's
journey from India! But something had happened to
the weather. The clear glare of the desert was hidden
by a curious mistiness. The sun looked like a white
ball in a thick grey sky; Sir Samuel thought it had the

dullness of a tennis ball. They nevertheless decided to take off, but rose almost immediately into a fearful violent duststorm raging through the atmosphere. In a few moments visibility was reduced to nothing in the swirling scorching dust, yet the gale-force wind buffeting the aircraft was bitingly cold. The pilot steered away from where he knew there were jagged mountains rising up from the coast, and flew out to sea to turn the aircraft and try to land again at Jask. The Hoares could see nothing except the dust, until suddenly the sea was below, ugly and grey, with uneasy white crested waves. Then they were over the sandy coast almost decapitating a party of Persians trekking along the shore on camels. A great double-winged aeroplane charging out of the screaming wind, the stinging blinding sand, the three engines thundering with the power of 1275 horses, the heavy rubber wheels just above the nomads' heads. The camels stampeded in terror. The aircraft regained height and landed back at Jask in minimal visibility. "We were much too interested to be frightened," said Lady Maude. They got out to find that the temperature had dropped from the extreme heat of the day before to intense cold, although the sand hitting their skins was scorching.

The rest of the day at the telegraph station manager's house was very tedious. They tried playing bridge but flies covered the numbers and flyspray made the cards sticky. Frequent visits to the station to read the telegrams about the storm revealed that it had spread over an enormous area.

But next day conditions improved and they made it, flying at 10,000 feet with the great solid yellow bank of dust below. Croydon to Karachi in 11 days. Sir Samuel felt certain that the route they had pioneered would one day be a great highway through the sky. In years to come the aeroplane, such an object of wonder on their journey, would be as ordinary and unexciting as the railway, the ship, the car and the bicycle.

The Hoares might fly to India in great style with a telegram of congratulation from King George V ("I hope that you and Lady Maude enjoyed your journey") and a state visit to a maharajah, with grouse shooting and tennis matches, but Imperial Airways did not actually get the Cairo–Karachi service functioning. The Hoares' flight was an official event, a "one-off" bonanza, courageous, exhilarating, and inaugural only in name. It was a grand tour in the new technology; showing the flag from the air. But the Persian government suddenly revoked its permission for Imperial Airways aeroplanes to fly along the northern side of the Gulf. German interests were gaining influence inside Persia. International politics were entangling with the granting of air routes. Imperial Airways had been carrying out secret negotiations with the Persians and now they had failed. The only alternative was flying along the southern shore of the Gulf. Imperial Airways were not interested because no communication facilities existed here, as on the north side, and there was a dangerous crossing over open sea from the Oman Promontory on the Arabian Peninsula to Baluchistan. So the new DH66s flew Cairo to Basra once a week like a stage-coach without the next stage, carrying mail, some passengers, and cargoes of small light things like medical supplies, gold bullion, precious stones, machinery parts, newspapers and samples of ladies' dresses.

Actual passengers had a more prosaic and perhaps more adventurous experience than the Hoares. The western terminus of the route was in fact an old hangar and a large shed with a marked-out area

of sand on the landing ground at Heliopolis, in the
suburbs of Cairo. It was impossible to continue the
flight through to London. Passengers had to travel by
train or car from Cairo to the Egyptian port of
Alexandria and catch a P & O liner across the
Mediterranean. The British had no commercial flying
boat capable of crossing the Mediterranean in 1927
and landplanes were considered too dangerous. The
Hoares had done it but that was an exception. Once
berthed on the European side of the Mediterranean,
unlike Sir Samuel and Lady Maude, passengers
caught trains. Aeroplanes could perfectly easily fly
across Europe, but the various governments bickering
down below on this smallish piece of earth could not
agree to allow landing rights and air routes.

8

Solo Flying

A COLD, DAMP, MISTY TUESDAY MORNING, Croydon Airport, 7 February 1928. A quiet, small, rather secretive Australian airman climbed into the cockpit of his single-engined Avro Avian. Bert Hinkler, test pilot, veteran of air races and international competitions, holder of the world long-distance record for a non-stop flight in a light aeroplane, intended to fly home to Australia. Hinkler was not flying because of any government schemes for a long-haul commercial air route from London to Australia. He was not flying in the wake of the frenzy for record-breaking flights in small aeroplanes that had erupted since the American Charles Lindbergh flew non-stop across the Atlantic in May 1927. Lindbergh had flown solo for 33 hours 39 minutes, with no way of seeing forward past the petrol tanks in his Ryan monoplane, except by raising a periscope. Hinkler was flying because he had wanted to make this journey ever since the war, and he believed he now had an aircraft capable of achieving the distance. His inspiration went back to the First World War when young Australians, trained to fly in Europe and the Middle East, dreamed of bringing their machines home, all the way across the

Bert Hinkler in the single-seater Sopwith *Dove*, April 1919
(E. A. Crome)

world. Hinkler had not managed to compete in the England–Australia Air Race in 1919, but his ambition, polished by constant flying, had been kept in harness waiting for the opportunity.

Very few aviators had managed to fly from England to Australia and no-one had broken the Smiths' time of 27 days 20 hours made in 1919. The only other crew to complete the course of the Air Race took seven months, arriving in Darwin in August 1920. Alan Cobham plus a mechanic flew from England to Australia in 36 days in 1926, with a 385-horsepower engine. Captain Lancaster and Mrs Miller left England in October 1927 in an Avro Avian, as did a formation flight of four RAF Supermarine *Southampton* flying boats on an unhurried goodwill and survey cruise. All were still on the way four months later in February 1928 when Bert Hinkler departed from Croydon.

Flying to Australia was still considered to be a massive challenge. Hinkler was the first to tackle it solo—no navigator, no mechanic—and he could not get newspaper or financial backing for what people considered a dangerous and stupid plan. "The response was about as good as if I had been trying to sell rotten fruit." The Avro Avian with its nine-metre (30-foot) wingspan was similar in weight and size to First World War fighter and reconnaissance planes. But Hinkler had an extra fuel tank built into the passenger seat giving him 300 litres (66 gallons), and the Cirrus 11 engine, although only 85 horsepower, was a great deal more reliable than those of 10 years before.

Hinkler intended breaking the Smiths' record. The first day was vital: a good long leap, a running start, to get as far as possible. Hinkler managed to travel from London to Rome, $12\frac{3}{4}$ hours' flying and a night landing, and nearly the end of the whole trip because he came down by mistake on one of Mussolini's military aerodromes and was locked up under guard. He chopped time and distance by not flying the established route across the Mediterranean, and by ignoring the desert route which was longer though much safer than the way he planned to go. He slept alone out in the desert by his aeroplane or in convivial RAF messes. During the flight down the Persian Gulf exhaustion drugged his responses, depressed his spirits and made him feel appallingly alone. He gave himself no days off to rest or overhaul the Avian's engine, but worked on it after every day's flying, grabbing a few hours' sleep before getting up again at dawn for the next day's flying. He pushed across India by a more direct route than other aviators, tackling wild mountainous country, sitting out a hammering, searing headache as the hot sun beat down and the noise of the engine nearly drove his tired brain demented.

Hinkler was an excellent navigator. His only maps were the relevant pages from the *Times Atlas of the World*. The scale diminished the further east he went until he was flying around one hour per two to three centimetres of map. But at least he experienced reasonable weather with not much fog and fairly isolated storms in the monsoon area. The heat had been the greatest problem: flying in the open cockpit his face cracked and blistered from the sun. His light aircraft managed the restricted spaces and muddy surfaces of temporary landing grounds better than the heavy Vimy.

Hinkler cut out two stops made by the Smiths in the Dutch East Indies and risked crossing more of the Timor Sea than they had. But he made it into Darwin in the late afternoon of Wednesday 22 February, after $10\frac{1}{2}$ hours non-stop in the air; a tired, hungry, unshaven man wearing the same double-breasted English woollen suit that he was wearing when he climbed into the cockpit at Croydon. He hadn't brought any change of clothing with him at all. But he had left London only 15½ days ago. No-one had ever travelled so far in such a short time.

Still infinitely weary after the physical and mental strain of the flight, Hinkler left Darwin on Friday and flew on down the Telegraph Line, then branched off to the south-east. After flying for more than nine hours in oppressive heat he landed by a windmill to have a drink. The bore water pumped from deep under ground probably made him ill. Hinkler inflated the rubber dinghy packed in a special compartment behind the cockpit for emergency use, and slept on it out in the silent empty outback. Just two weeks ago he had used the dinghy for a bed in the Libyan desert in Africa. Nomadic Arabs armed with knives and rifles had found him there and helped him clear camel-thorn bushes so he could get a clear enough run to take off. Here in the Northern Territory one Aborigine walked past him. Worried officials instituted a search because he had failed to arrive where he was expected. Hinkler had not yet realised that his landing places were world news.

Next morning he flew on, linking up with the Qantas route. The citizens of Longreach were finding themselves well placed to view champion long-distance aviators, but they were becoming rather casual about the experience. When Hinkler arrived on the Sunday, one souvenir hunter immediately snatched off his goggles, and women sat their babies on the Avian's vulnerable fabric wings.

On Monday afternoon Hinkler landed in Bundaberg to an overwhelming exuberant welcome. The Controller of Civil Aviation, Colonel H. C. Brinsmead, gave a speech at the civic reception. "Aviation is just about at the turning of the ways," he told Hinkler. "The dark days of experiment, research, partial failure and complete failure are merging into partial success and I hope that the days of complete success are not far distant."

Toasts were drunk, champagne flowed, cigar smoke rose, politicians made speeches. A long trail of public functions stretched ahead of Hinkler the home-grown hero. Crowds collected wherever he went, schoolchildren were given half-day holidays to see him. His extraordinary, courageous flight brought him fame, prizes, world renown. The Australian government decided that it was not a stunt, or a freak, and presented him with quite a large sum of money. But Bert Hinkler had made the flight not for any of these rewards; he flew from England to Australia because he wanted to.

There was an unexpected repercussion. Hinkler had dared to attempt the route solo in a small landplane. It *was* possible to grind across those huge distances, and quickly. Hinkler's flight helped unleash a race for the fastest time between England and Australia, a race which became relentless, almost manic, and destroyed great airmen, including Bert Hinkler himself.

Aviators had reached out for records from the beginning: the furthest, highest, fastest flight, the first across the Channel, across mountains, the first across the United States, the first around the world. Prizes were there to be won and aviators tried for whatever challenge was on offer. Specially designed machines were built to make attempts on records; clubs and societies were formed to encourage the "sport" of flying. A small coterie of experienced pilots, or the members of the various air forces, pushed against the edges of a human's ability to stay in the air.

But after Charles Lindbergh's flight across the Atlantic in May 1927 a new kind of record-breaking began. Lindbergh was tall and handsome and the public treated him as a hero. Record-breaking aviators could experience the fame and publicity usually reserved for filmstars and top sportspeople. Wealth and public adoration seemed to await the successful performer in the long-distance flying stakes. This was not the world of experts and official clubs any longer. The doings of top aviators made endless newspaper copy. Lindbergh was the first to fly non-stop across the Atlantic since Alcock and Brown in 1919, yet within weeks of his achievement pilots began throwing themselves at the challenge to beat his time with disastrous results. At the end of June 1927 two experienced United States naval lieutenants managed to achieve the first non-stop flight from San Francisco out into the Pacific to Hawaii. Immediately an air race was organised to beat the time and 10 people lost their lives in the mad scramble and subsequent searches for lost planes. Light aeroplanes had been designed, capable of being flown long distances, single-handed, and they were being flown. Amateurs could fly and they did. Titled English ladies made solo journeys to distant parts of the Empire: women had flown from the beginning but the First World War coming so early in aviation's development helped fix it as a male profession, and women tended to need independent income or some social freedom to break through into flying.

People set out on ever more daring or dangerous attempts, often ill prepared. There were crashes and disappearances—pointless tragedies. The whole phenomenon was severely criticised. But for many of the public, record-breaking seemed an extension of the flying circuses—the double excitement of amazing achievements and disastrous crashes, the double anticipation of success to wonder at and the shock of failure. "It was a record-breaking time when a new record got your name in the papers, and generally made a success of you," said Australian Charles Kingsford Smith. Kingsford Smith and his companion Charles Ulm wanted to fly across the Pacific Ocean, but first they reckoned they had to tackle some smaller, minor record and leapfrog from that to the backing necessary for the Pacific attempt. "We wanted fame, money, status," said Kingsford Smith, "but we were not known as airmen." He had learned to fly in the war, stunted for film-makers in Hollywood, worked for flying circuses, and done two years' commercial flying on the long Western Australian Airways route. Ulm did not actually hold a pilot's licence. In June 1927 the two men broke their minor record—the fastest flight around Australia—got some financial support and left for California to prepare for the attempt on the Pacific. When, with a crew of radio operator and navigator, they took their three-engined Fokker F.VIIB-3m *Southern Cross* from San Francisco to Brisbane in three mammoth non-stop flights, from 31 May to 9 June 1928, they received all the adulation, money and fame their great achievement could win.

The months in America had been heavy with financial struggle and near failure. Buying and fitting out the Fokker was terribly expensive, but the Australians soon realised that only a large, powerful, specially strengthened aircraft could tackle what most people regarded as a suicide attempt. *Southern Cross* was equipped with the latest navigating instruments, and radios, and Kingsford Smith trained himself in the techniques of flying at night and flying blind through bad weather using the unfamiliar instruments installed in the cockpit.

Once in Australia Kingsford Smith and Ulm planned attempts on a sheaf of records. *Southern Cross* was one of the biggest best-equipped aircraft seen in Australia. They flew non-stop from an RAAF base near Melbourne to Perth as a warm-up, then managed a terrifying storm-racked crossing of the Tasman Sea between Australia and New Zealand, the first aeroplane to make the distance safely, but only just: death came close during the night. The return journey from New Zealand against a headwind took over 23 hours. *Southern Cross* made a night landing at Richmond aerodrome outside Sydney with the help of specially set up floodlights, flares and the headlights of hundreds of cars.

How quickly could the big three-engined Fokker fly the air route from Australia to England? Planning the flight took a long time: petrol had to be ready at stopovers, permits and permission were needed for landing and taking off in foreign countries, *Southern Cross*'s three engines had to be thoroughly overhauled. Kingsford Smith and Ulm decided to ignore the usual route through Queensland and over to Darwin. *Southern Cross* had the petrol capacity to fly diagonally across the centre of Australia, Sydney non-stop to the little port of Wyndham up on the remote north-west coast of the continent. Flying over the huge stretches of outback Australia, the scrub and the waterless desert, would not be nearly as worrying, they reckoned, as the kind of flying they had experienced over open ocean.

The deep wicker chairs in the cockpit were familiar, even comforting, as Kingsford Smith and Ulm settled into them late in the morning of 31 March 1929. They had spent so much time here, and they

Charles Ulm (left) and Charles Kingsford Smith in flying gear
(Qantas Collection)

trusted and knew their machine. Navigator H. A. Litchfield and radio operator T. H. McWilliams were at work in the little equipment-filled cabin which was just large enough to stand in, and long enough to lie on the floor and rest, if necessary. A big fuel tank seeping its petrol fumes into the cabin blocked all access to the cockpit. Litchfield and McWilliams could only communicate with Kingsford Smith and Ulm by poking a note pinned to the end of a stick through the gap. In the cockpit the noise of the three engines was so overpowering the two pilots had to nudge, or point, or write notes—the loudest shout could not be heard.

In the middle of the night, after crossing the Overland Telegraph Line, the weather suddenly deteriorated. Rain came slamming in on great gusts of wind, jolting and rocking the aircraft. Nothing could be seen beyond the torrential rain lashing down, hour after hour. Kingsford Smith was at the controls, flying by instruments. He was highly experienced at blind flying but it was a tiring nerve-racking business. Dawn only turned the blackness, through which they could see nothing, into greyness. Gradually the rain eased and they caught glimpses of the country below: rough, ravine-scarred, heavily timbered, utterly inhospitable looking. They followed a long ravine west towards the sea expecting to find Wyndham at the end. All they found was an angry ocean beating in on cliffs. The bad conditions during the night had meant Litchfield had made no sightings to fix their position. An accident soon after leaving Sydney to the long-range aerial, a wire on a reel trailing 50 metres (150 feet) beneath the fuselage, meant they could not receive signals. Their only map of the area was from the *Times Atlas* and they could recognise no features.

For the next five or six hours they flew along the deeply indented coastline of this remote corner of Australia searching for Wyndham, but doubling back because they misunderstood the signals made by Aborigines at a mission station, then back over their tracks again, across appalling wild country in abominable weather, lost, completely lost. They found the huts of another mission station. In response to a note dropped with a weight attached, they were shown a new direction for Wyndham. They set out, but their petrol was failing so they turned back to try and make a forced landing by the mission. At least even if they were injured in the landing they could get help and eventually make contact with the outside world. But in that terrible country with visibility still poor they could not find the roofs of the mission station again. Kingsford Smith saw a swampy mudflat at the head of an inlet and brought *Southern Cross* down. The wheels sank into the mud slowing the great machine, she tilted forward, then came to a halt. No-one was injured. They had been $28\frac{1}{2}$ hours in the air and it was the evening of 1 April. They had no idea in which direction the mission station lay. Mosquitoes swarmed in black clouds and bit them mercilessly.

Next morning the flies took over from the mosquitoes, but the sun came out drying the mud and Litchfield was able to take sights which established their position accurately: 240 kilometres (150 miles) short of Wyndham and 24 kilometres (15 miles) from the coast, near the Glenelg River. The young English explorer George Grey, landing close to here almost 100 years ago eager to discover great things for Britain, named what he thought might be a great river for Lord Glenelg. Grey nearly died from exhaustion clambering over the appalling terrain and from injuries after being speared by an Aborigine. The two mission stations Kingsford Smith and Ulm had seen from the air were not marked on any charts. The area seemed as empty and remote as when Grey first discovered it.

The airmen decided to wait by *Southern Cross*.
It seemed a kind of home in this ghastly place. At least
they had plenty of water to drink, and for a while they
divided up a consignment of baby food they were
meant to be delivering in Wyndham. Their emergency
food supplies were unaccountably missing. As the days
went by, hunger made them weaker and more listless.
They could not catch fish and in any case crocodiles
patrolled the water. They tried eating nauseous mud-
flavoured snails that crawled up the mangrove trees
out of the tide's reach. The flies plagued them during
the day and the mosquitoes tortured them at night,
lack of cigarettes made them bad tempered, the heat
was relentless. The big storm had been the last of the
monsoon rain and now the country was drying out,
but the mud was too sticky to allow a take-off. In any
case they had no petrol. Every day they staggered up a
nearby hill to keep a signal fire alight, but the wood
was green and burnt meanly and the effort exhausted
them. They could listen on their short-wave radio and
hear about the searches being made for them, but they
could not get a radio transmitter working. Would they
ever be seen? Several searching aeroplanes passed in
the distance and failed to notice *Southern Cross*.

Search aircraft setting out from Melbourne and
Sydney had to get right across Australia before they
could even start looking for the downed *Southern
Cross*. For all anyone knew the four men were dead.
Petrol companies struggled to rush supplies to remote
depots. The airmen's old friend Keith Anderson set out
with his mechanic Bobby Hitchcock in his small light
aeroplane *Kookaburra* on an independent search,
but disappeared west of the Telegraph Line. Engine
trouble forced them down in rough desert country
and both men perished of thirst.

Australia's vast spaces were ill mapped and
communications facilities for aircraft were non-

existent. There was no organisation for meteorological information, no navigational aids. Anyone force-landing away from the few established routes faced heavy risks. The continent might seem ideal for aeroplanes but there were huge areas of wild difficult country where a downed machine could stay lost, and vast dry areas where lost men died quickly. Anderson and Hitchcock had even drunk the fluid from their compass in their extremity. "I knew the high desert country they had come down in was so dry at this period of the year even the Aborigines had moved out," said Qantas pilot Lester Brain, who eventually found Anderson's aeroplane.

Southern Cross was discovered on the twelfth day of searching by a specially chartered DH66. The four crew members were exhausted and weakened by hunger. The radio operator of the DH66 described the area of the Kimberleys they had been combing as "indescribably dreadful, and we were careful to carry an experienced bushman with us in case we were forced down and would have to make our way back to civilisation. Enormous rivers and estuaries, where the tide rose and fell 40 feet [13 metres], were intermingled with great mudflats, precipitous canyons, high hills and wild bush country. To speak of this region being charted on the map is absurd. It would be almost impossible for the most skilful surveyor to map this wild, rugged and inaccessible district." (Charles Kingsford Smith, *My Flying Life*, Andrew Melrose Ltd, 1937, page 110)

One of the world's best-equipped aircraft, and another flown by an experienced pilot, had come to grief all too easily flying an unfamiliar route across the emptiness of the continent.

Within weeks a third aeroplane was missing in northern Australia. Two airmen, S. J. Moir and H. C. Owen, flying the England to Australia route in a

single-engine Vickers Vellore, vanished on the sixty-
first day of their journey during the Timor Sea
crossing. Qantas pilot Lester Brain went out searching.
It was no use looking at sea, he reckoned. They had
been missing five days. He did not have the range to
fly over the Timor Sea to find out if the airmen had
turned back part-way across. The only hope was to
search along the coast in case they had reached the
mainland. Brain flew east over Arnhem Land, then
turned back along the coast. An isolated lighthouse
stood amongst the scrub at Cape Don, with no radio or
telephone, supplied twice a year by ship. As he neared
the lighthouse Brain saw the wreckage of an aeroplane. There was nowhere possible to land so he threw
down a stone with a note wrapped around it. If the
airmen are alive put one white sheet out on the
ground, if dead put two. Little figures rushed out and
the message came: one white sheet. Are they injured,
do they need a doctor? Yes, one white sheet; no, two
sheets. The answer—one white sheet. Brain realised
that he did not know if the airmen were still actually at
the lighthouse—they might have already left by boat
for Darwin. This method of communicating left enormous gaps. He dropped a last paper-wrapped stone:
do you want a boat to pick them up? Yes, one white
sheet—and the sheet was laid out again. Brain flew
back to Darwin with the good news and the injured
men were collected by sea.

The north coast was the only jumping-off and
landing place for aircraft in Australia and it was a
dangerous and remote place to use. The disaster of
Southern Cross's forced landing, and the deaths of
Anderson and Hitchcock, were examined in detail by a
committee of enquiry. There were rumours that the
forced landing had been planned as a publicity stunt.
The day after the report clearing them was made

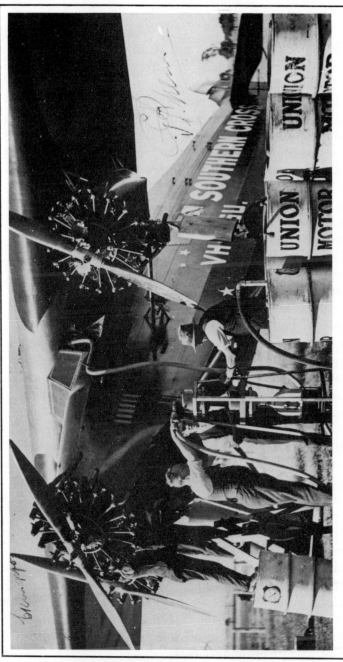

Southern Cross refuelling at Richmond, New South Wales, before taking off on the second attempt to fly to England, 25 June 1929 (Qantas Collection)

public Kingsford Smith and Ulm, Litchfield and
McWilliams set out again for England. Repairs had
been made to *Southern Cross* because the long expo-
sure to the weather had caused timbers to warp and
the fabric covering to deteriorate. An emergency radio
transmitter that could work on the ground was carried, more tools, plenty of emergency rations, water,
flares, a shotgun. The only thing forgotten was cotton-
wool, and Kingsford Smith and Ulm arrived at Derby,
down the coast from Wyndham, stone-deaf from
engine noise. Three thousand two hundred and twenty
kilometres (2000 miles) non-stop in 22 hours. *Southern Cross* left Derby on 27 June 1929 and flew on to
Singapore, the first aircraft to make the journey
non-stop, then on up the usual route, through monsoon storms, and heat, and duststorms, to the summer
weather of Europe. The engines were giving trouble.
They were not allowed to land at Rangoon when they
planned on the Saturday because of the races; in
Calcutta a long bamboo stake driven into the ground
tore a great gash into the underbody as they were
taking off; and in Athens they were refused permission
to depart because they lacked the necessary papers.
But they reached England in 12 days 18 hours, the
fastest time ever, but not breaking Bert Hinkler's
record because that had been made solo in a single-
engined light aeroplane.

It was almost 10 years since Ross and Keith
Smith pioneered the route in the Vickers Vimy. Now
in mid-1929 a three-engined monoplane, equipped
like the Vimy with four crew and long-range tanks,
had managed the distance between England and
Australia in less than two weeks, including delays.
Like all the record-breaking machines, *Southern
Cross* was making a one-off journey, and carried no
payload except crew and fuel.

9

The Route Develops

SMOKING WAS PERMITTED IN THE CABIN of Imperial Airways' new flying boat built especially for carrying passengers across the Mediterranean. Petrol was stored in the wings set high above the boat-shaped fuselage, so people could puff in safety. The new Short Calcuttas were also built almost entirely of metal, a first for British commercial flying. With an open cockpit for the pilot and seating for 16 passengers, the Calcuttas were Imperial Airways' first flying boats capable of crossing a large stretch of water. The three Bristol Jupiter 500-horsepower engines were suspended between the biplane wings which seemed to tower over the boat-shaped hull in an unwieldy-looking structure.

The Calcuttas began service across the Mediterranean on the last day of March 1929 when the England to India air route finally opened. The Persians had relented and the DH66 Hercules pioneered by Sir Samuel and Lady Hoare were permitted to fly on down the Gulf and around to Karachi. The great imperial air route—the backbone from which would be hung all other routes—was functioning, once a week, at least for parcels and letters. No

Five Short S.8 Calcutta flying boats were built in 1928 to carry
Imperial Airways passengers and mail across the Mediterranean
Sea (RAF Museum, Hendon)

fare-paying passengers used it for several months.

While Imperial Airways aircraft hopped sedately and carefully along the England to India route, the German airship *Graf Zeppelin* was showing just what the latest rigid airship could do. *Graf Zeppelin*, a mighty silver monster, as long as the longest ocean liner, quietly and gently flew around the world in August 1929, from New Jersey, USA, to Germany, on to Tokyo, across the Pacific to Los Angeles and back to New Jersey, 33,800 kilometres (21,000 miles) in 21 days seven hours 34 minutes with only three intermediate stops. A crew of 42 maintained the airship during its three-week cruise. Twenty passengers enjoyed spacious accommodation: they sat down to meals on floral upholstered chairs in a wallpapered dining-room, read books and played cards in the saloon, and slept in comfortable double-berthed cabins, each with flowers in a vase on a lace-covered table. Airships did seem to many people in aviation to be the answer to long-haul passenger travel.

Work on the two British rigid airships, both over 200 metres (700 feet) long, was nearing completion. Would they take over from the flying boats and landplanes on the Empire routes? The enormous mooring tower and airship hangar were ready in Karachi. On 14 October 1929 the government-funded R101 staggered aloft on its first flight. Something was obviously wrong. Problems had beset this project from the beginning. The passenger accommodation was excellent but the airship was badly overweight and underpowered, and a decision was made after several more short flights to lengthen the framework and add more gas bags.

On the afternoon of 26 October one of the Short Calcutta flying boats working the Mediterra-

nean developed engine trouble off the Italian coast and
landed on the sea in a gale. The big flying boat slewed
and bounced unmanageably in the water as a tug
began towing it towards harbour. In the gathering
darkness the crew climbed out onto the wings to add
their weight to the problem of balancing the craft.
Suddenly the three towing cables snapped one after
the other. The flying boat capsized though no-one saw
it go, drowning the three crew and four passengers;
the mails were lost. The Short Calcuttas handled
poorly in the sea during rough weather.

　　　　A raging gale helped bring about the disastrous
crash of R101 during the early hours of Sunday 5
October 1930, near Beauvais, France. But the monster
airship had set out ill prepared and undertested on its
maiden voyage to India. R100, the Vickers airship
creatively designed by Barnes Wallis, had flown from
England to Canada and returned, only nine weeks
before, but it was eventually sawn up for scrap and
sold. In the tragedy of the R101 crash, and the ghastly
fire as the hydrogen in the huge gas bags exploded, all
British airship hopes were destroyed. Much vital de-
velopmental money went with them. British air routes
would now, without any more uncertainty, be flown
by landplanes and flying boats.

　　　　Fortunately Imperial Airways had two new
machines on order. One was a four-engined flying
boat, a new glamorous, more powerful machine from
Short's, the S.17 Kent, designed to take over from the
Calcuttas on the Mediterranean route. The other was
the "flying banana", the giant Handley Page HP42
airliner, a stately railway carriage of an aeroplane,
long body suspended beneath huge biplane wings;
unstreamlined, slow, old-fashioned at birth, but to be
much loved by passengers as the symbol of Imperial
Airways service. A corrugated-aluminium alloy skin

The British airship R101 tethered to its mooring tower
(RAF Museum, Hendon)

did cover the front two-thirds of the fuselage, but the
rest of the aeroplane was covered by the familiar sewn,
doped and varnished fabric. And the HP42 did have
an enclosed cockpit. Ever since Captain Hope
smashed away the experimental cockpit on the converted HP0/400 after the war Handley Page had
considered them dangerous. It also had a tail wheel
instead of a skid, and air brakes on the main wheels.
The cabin walls were lined, making it unnecessary to
stuff cottonwool in the ears to cut down the racket of
the engines, and it was quite easy to hear a conversa-
tion and talk, without shouting, across the aisle. There
was heating and individual air vents, two toilets,
steward service, and meals could be prepared in the
galley.

Up to 38 passengers travelled on the "Heracles" Class designed for European routes, and 24 on
the "Hannibal" Class designed for the long-haul
Empire routes. Passengers sat in either the forward or
aft cabins in comfortable, upholstered roomy chairs,
and looked out wide windows with pretty lace-edged
curtains.

The HP42 was a reliable traditional aircraft, an
opting for size and luxury at the expense of speed and
modern technology. As such it reflected the cautious,
conservative and complacent attitudes of Imperial
Airways. Important new ideas had been incorporated
into some European aircraft. Research and development in the United States was about to send American
aviation design surging ahead. The British seemed
content with small orders for hand-built machines of
proven construction. Only five Short Calcutta flying
boats were ever built, three Kents, and eight HP42s.

The Kents and Handley Pages helped improve
the England to India journey but route-making was
turning out to be a complicated, slow business. Flying

SEATING PLAN OF AN AIRLINER
OF THE HERACLES CLASS

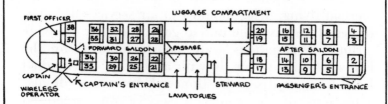

SEATING PLAN OF AN AIRLINER
OF THE HANNIBAL CLASS

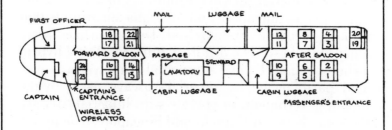

Imperial Airways' HP42 Heracles Class aircraft carried up to 38
passengers on the European routes, while the Hannibal Class
catered for 24 passengers on the Empire routes
(British Airways)

on from Karachi into India was not a straightforward
matter of extending the air route because the Indian
government wished to share in decisions about commercial flying. Who should run air services in India:
Imperial Airways, the Indian government or a private
airline? Negotiations were poorly handled by the
British. "Who'd ever fly with an Indian?" remarked
Lord Chetwynd sent by Imperial Airways to discuss
extensions of the route. A service was organised
between Karachi and Delhi with crews and aeroplanes
chartered from Imperial Airways. The Indian government surveyed a route through to Rangoon and built
all-weather airfields, but the Depression limited the
money available. The Indians were uncooperative
towards Imperial Airways' ambitions to use the route
and get on to Singapore and Australia, an attitude that
rankled because French and Dutch airlines were
allowed to do so. The deadlock unfroze when a hybrid
airline, Indian Trans-Continental Airways, was created, partly owned by Imperial Airways, partly by the
Indian government, to operate with Imperial Airways
the route between Karachi and Singapore. The jigsaw
pieces fell into place during 1933.

    The route down the Gulf functioned for two
years; then the Persian government informed Imperial
Airways in 1931 that they had decided on a new air
route inland, away from the coast. It included high
mountains, salt deserts, built-in sandstorms and some
jungle. The British, concerned about their position in
Persia, had in the meantime begun long and delicately
negotiated treaties with the sheiks on the southern side
of the Gulf. The necessary wireless and telegraph
stations were being established. HP42 Hannibals with
their range of 930 kilometres (580 miles) could
manage the worrying sea crossing from the bottom of
the Gulf over to the mainland of Baluchistan, although

The HP42 Hannibal at Bahrain en route to India (Courtesy of BAPCO, Bahrain)

Imperial Airways would have preferred using flying boats. No suitable harbours could be found, however. Sites for airfields were not easy to choose either, but the Isle of Bahrain where oil had just been discovered was decided on, and Sharjah in the desert, on the western coast of the rugged Arabian Peninsula. In October 1932 Imperial Airways shifted out of Persia and into the friendlier territories of the sheiks of the Trucial coast.

The European section of the route was messy. Restrictions by foreign governments on British aircraft meant that the jigsaw pieces of route were fiddled into new combinations then broken up and rearranged. Passengers travelled by plane and train, at times via the Balkans, depending on the season of the year, the weather, the hours of daylight available and the state of British disputes over reciprocity with France, Germany, Italy and Greece. From October 1931 all passengers for the Mediterranean and beyond flew between London and Paris then travelled by train two nights and a day from Paris to the port of Brindisi in south-east Italy. Quite apart from problems with the governments concerned it was in fact cheaper and easier for Imperial Airways to move its passengers that way. But it meant that the Empire air routes did not include an aeroplane flight where it might have been most expected—over Europe. Despite its great aims and its need to represent British prestige abroad Imperial Airways was still a struggling airline with barely enough aircraft to keep services running, over-extended on its routes and undercapitalised. At the end of 1932, for example, it had 32 aircraft employed in regular air transport and a third of those were the new HP42s and Short Kents. France had, according to the head of Imperial Airways in a letter to the *Daily Mail*, 269 aircraft and Germany 177. Imperial had 32 pilots compared with 135 French and 160 German, and flew one-third of the average weekly French distances, and one-eighth of the German.

Imperial Airways had got government interference in exchange for its subsidy, and insufficient investment from its private funding. Competition from European airlines helped drive it from European routes but failed to shake a complacent and sometimes arrogant attitude towards businesslike speed on the Empire routes. As the "government" airline it got caught up in problems with foreign powers, and developed a secretiveness about revealing plans. As the "government" airline it had to face opposition to its purpose and very existence from politicians and civil servants in London.

Not many people risked travelling by air between England and India. Civil servants made quick journeys back to England for long-service leave, oil men flew to the Gulf, army officers took up postings on the frontiers of the Empire. Only 75 fare-paying passengers flew the route in 1932, and 46 in 1933. The French and Dutch were providing a faster, more competitive service. To the general public long-distance flying was still a kind of stunt. The European routes were pleasant and reliable enough, but beyond Europe flying was an adventure with definite risks. There were no regulations, for example, about how much fuel an Imperial Airways aircraft should carry and passengers could find themselves landing unexpectedly in the desert to take on some more fuel. The pilots of the prestigious Handley Pages even on occasion misjudged the fuel required for the two-hour 15-minute flight from London to Paris and landed on the coast for a refill. Out on the imperial routes engine failure could occur in bandit-ridden country. Pot-shots could still be taken at passing planes. Accom-

The interior of a DH61 biplane, the first Qantas aircraft fitted with a toilet, 1929 (Qantas Collection)

modation varied. Halfway across the desert route at
Rutbah Wells a romantic-looking fort had been specially built. At night the gate clanged shut against the
threat of marauding Arabs. Ten years ago hardly any
Europeans had been seen in these deserts. Now
travellers from around the world gathered at the
guesthouse dining table and swapped tales before
going to bed.

Passengers travelling outback Queensland
routes with Qantas in 1929 experienced the pleasure
of the first inflight toilet on a scheduled air service in
Australia. No longer was an agonised sprint to the
little tin shed in the corner of the airfield necessary.
Qantas added two DH61 biplanes equipped with the
new convenience to their fleet, plus room for seven or
eight passengers. Stories of empty jam-jars for
emergency use began to belong to the past; or of the
big rum-drinking blacksmith Darky Rawlins who,
desperate to relieve himself, tried to push open the
cabin door during one flight, then carefully filled both
elastic-sided riding boots and gave them to the pilot on
landing.

Qantas' routes had been extended to the mining town of Mount Isa, to Camooweal on the Northern
Territory border, and up to Normanton on the Gulf of
Carpentaria. But Qantas wanted a base in the Queensland capital, Brisbane. They won the right to a
subsidised airmail link between their outback route
and Brisbane in 1928, and Alexander Kennedy, now
91 years old, was a passenger on the inaugural flight
up to Charleville, on 17 April 1929. A new DH61
opened the once-weekly service travelling at an average speed of 156 kilometres per hour (97 miles per
hour).

Qantas was a sturdy enough little airline, but it
still needed to pioneer the idea of flying to an uncer-

tain public. "Sit at ease in the machine; your move-
ments cannot possibly affect its balance", stated a
leaflet of advice. Passengers, mail and freight did not
overburden the routes. Essential extra revenue still
came from air-taxi and ambulance work, and joy-
rides. Pilot Lester Brain was stationed in Brisbane in
1927, running a flying school for the company
teaching people how to fly in the new light aeroplanes.
He hired himself and a Gipsy Moth out to whoever
would pay—wheeler-dealer cattle men, photographers
wanting aerial views and press shots. On weekends he
barnstormed country towns, or the beaches, selling
four-minute rides. The Moth took off at low tide along
the hard sand and at high tide Brain pulled it up into
the sand hills and went surfing.

Pilots working the outback route were getting
used to flying through the poor visibility of dust.
Drought was drying out the centre and winds lifted
and sifted broken-down soil into a gritty haze. There
were no maps, no radio, no weather reports, no blind
flying instruments nor training in blind flying. It was
visual flying and that meant knowing the country like
the palm of your hand, every gate and fence and the
layout of each homestead as you went over, counting
them off, knowing the shape of dry river channels and
the direction and position of bushtracks. The pilots
acted as agents for tickets and freight, as baggage and
passenger handlers and as cleaners if anyone had been
sick during a flight. They acted as middlemen between
the aeroplane and the public's grasp of what this new
technology could do for them. The Qantas route could
mean blocks of ice and fresh butter in hot Camooweal
where there were no refrigerators. Once in the early
days of Qantas Hudson Fysh had found live fish
struggling in the street. A freak rainstorm had whirled
them up out of their watery home and deposited them,

after who knew how long a journey, in dusty Longreach. Now Qantas aeroplanes carried sacks of barra-
mundi from the Gulf down to inland towns, and the
fish arrived still feebly flapping.

In 1928, after years of discussions between
Hudson Fysh and Rev. John Flynn, Qantas contracted
to supply a DH50A converted to ambulance work for
use in an Aerial Medical Service—the beginning of
what became the Flying Doctor Service. Qantas aeroplanes had from the start flown sick people from
isolated back country into town for medical attention.
Now a regular service began, based in Cloncurry, and
all surrounding stations were sent a circular on "How
to Make Your Own Landing Ground, and How to
Receive an Aeroplane".

By 1930 Qantas had flown a million miles (1.6
million kilometres), all within the State of Queensland, and had a fleet of single-engined biplanes of
varying ages. Other airline companies with interstate
routes and some impressive new big multi-engined
aircraft were pushing for dominance in Australia. Not
all could survive economically, particularly with the
Depression reducing available spending power. The
prize, which would knock out the unlucky and boost
the successful, was the right to carry overseas airmail.
Hudson Fysh was determined that any England–
Australia airmail service would enter Australia at
Darwin and come down the Qantas route to the
eastern States. But Qantas had some determined
opponents. The battle was to fill the next years. They
were years of anxious negotiating, lobbying, propaganda—a war of manoeuvre and nerves, as Fysh
described it—which delayed rather than speeded up
the placing of the final jigsaw pieces in the long air
route between England and Australia.

In the meantime aviators kept on tackling this

longest challenge, this bizarre across-the-world flight.
Moir and Owen had crashlanded at Cape Don in 1929,
61 days from England. Francis Chichester made it in a
Moth in $36\frac{1}{2}$ days in January 1930. Piper and
Kaye took 42 days in March. No Australian aircraft
flew commercially outside Australia. No British commercial aircraft flew beyond India. Yet the England—
Australia air route existed, a notorious, dangerous
possibility to the seekers after fame, the record-
breakers.

10

Record-breaking Flights

I HAVE NO MONEY AND NO INFLUENCE.

I want to fly to Australia, one reason being that I am certain a successful flight of this nature, by an English girl, solo and in a light 'plane, would do much to engender confidence amongst the public in air travel ...

By my own efforts, and through many difficulties, I have trained myself for a career in Aviation ... I am getting rather desperate about this matter of raising finance and I cannot do anything worthwhile without it ...

I shall be deeply grateful if you can do anything at all to help me. Just a reply to my letter would encourage me to further efforts.

Yours truly

... and then a blank. Sir Sefton Brancker received many unsolicited letters but the writer of this one had forgotten to sign her name.

Amy Johnson had written hundreds of begging letters—to peers, newspaper proprietors, public figures—and got no replies or polite good wishes. But Sir Sefton Brancker followed her letter up and organised an introduction to the oil magnate Lord Wakefield, who promised to supply fuel along the

route and share the cost of an aeroplane with her
father.

With the necessary financial backing now se-
cured, Amy Johnson bought a secondhand Gipsy
Moth already fitted with long-range tanks giving it a
potential duration in the air of 13 hours. She had it
painted bottle-green with silver lettering, and christ-
ened it *Jason*. A sturdy two-seater wood and fabric
biplane, the Moth had a single 100-horsepower engine, and was almost the same size and weight as an
Avro Avian. The top of the cockpit reached about
shoulder height, the sturdy wings spanned nine metres
(30 feet). The cockpit was fitted with an airspeed
indicator, altimeter, turn-and-bank indicator and one
compass. Amy packed everything she thought she
might need into the front cockpit and fitted a cover
over it. There were tools and spares, a sun-helmet and
mosquito net, cooking stove and billy cans, medicines
and a revolver. An extra propeller was lashed to the
side of the fuselage. She hadn't been able to find out
much about conditions along the way. When, for
example, would the monsoon begin? No-one she asked
seemed to know. On the other hand she had decided to
disregard the conventional route as far as Baghdad.
According to the map the shortest distance to the
Persian Gulf seemed to be via Vienna and Constantinople, keeping east of the Mediterranean, and flying
over wild mountainous regions of Turkey. Enthusiastic, determined, in many ways ignorant and innocent
of the hazards, she decided to tackle this innovation.
Travelling 1300 kilometres (800 miles) a day, she
would be in Australia in 12 days.

Amy Johnson used the fact of being female to
try to get what she needed to carry out the flight, but
she did not have many other cards to play. Her
strongest card was her mechanical ability. She was the

Amy Johnson, "British Girl Flyer" (RAF Museum, Hendon)

second woman in England to hold a ground engineer's
licence. It had taken real determination plus courage
to counter prejudice and pass the exams. For a time
she was the only woman in the world to hold a valid
licence. But she had been flying solo for just six
months when she began pushing for financial assistance from anyone willing to back her attempt to beat
Bert Hinkler's time. A dramatic record flight would
bring her publicity and money, and launch her in her
chosen career, she believed. The England–Australia
route had such a strong hold on public imagination it
was the obvious choice. It was glamorous, dangerous,
exotic. And it was the furthest anyone could attempt to
fly in a light aeroplane. "I was told hair-raising
stories," said Amy Johnson, "of torture-loving bandits
in the mountain vastnesses of Turkey and Iraq, of wild
beasts in the desert and jungle, of cannibals in the
farther islands of the East Indies, and of sharks in the
Timor Sea." She was willing to tackle the flight with
little preparation and minimal experience compared
with the aviators who had achieved the great pioneer
flights.

But Amy Johnson belonged to a new genera-
tion. She was born the year the Wright brothers
managed powered flight and she grew up knowing
that aeroplanes were capable of travelling long distances. She was 16 when Alcock and Brown crossed
the Atlantic and Ross and Keith Smith got through to
Australia. She never experienced the wonder that the
miracle of flight had been achieved. An older aviator
like Bert Hinkler marvelled at the first successes. He
built a glider in a small Queensland town after
thinking through the theory of flight, reading all he
could in magazines, and learning mechanics by correspondence. Hinkler came to England in 1913 aged 21

because he hoped to learn more about the new world of aviation there than he could in Australia. Amy Johnson at the same age had never considered flying. She decided to learn the year Hinkler flew to Australia because flying in light aeroplanes was a fashionable, exciting and pleasurable sport in the late 1920s, although unusual for a woman. It was easy enough for her to go along to a flying club in north London and put her name down on the waiting list for lessons. A half-hour flying lesson cost one-tenth of her weekly salary and she managed to save enough for a lesson every two weeks. Flying was an expensive hobby but once having begun, she was a determined and dedicated learner. Amy Johnson's was the genera-tion of the light aeroplane club, the civilian, the private flier, the amateur. Aviation was still romantic and adventurous. But her initiation into the world of aeroplanes began 10 years after the end of the First World War with its intense flying and survive-or-die pilots.

Three hectic weeks after her introduction to Lord Wakefield, Amy Johnson was at Croydon pre-paring for take-off. To reassure her parents she was wearing a parachute strapped over her fur-collared Sidcot suit, but it was awkwardly suspended under her bottom. At least it could double as a cushion. Her aeroplane was a ponderous, unwieldy weight. Amy had never taken off heavily loaded and she failed at the first attempt. She had owned the Moth two weeks and flown it twice, her longest-ever flight had been London home to Hull, 240 kilometres (150 miles) in two hours 10 minutes. She had never flown an aeroplane out of England.

Then at the second attempt she was away, a small figure in a small aeroplane, a speck disappearing

into the mistiness of a cold morning, Monday 5 May
1930. Her family and friends waiting in England
would not know if she had survived each day until she
landed somewhere and sent off a cable. The cables
came—from Vienna, 1250 kilometres (775 miles),
from Constantinople, 1290 kilometres (800 miles),
Aleppo, 925 kilometres (575 miles). She was making
good time, but she was having hair-raising escapes.

Outside Baghdad Amy flew into a duststorm.
Before she knew what was happening the aircraft
lurched sickeningly and dropped several thousand
feet. The propeller stopped, restarted, but again she
plummeted down, in the control of some terrible force.
Dust caked her goggles, her eyes stung. She was
terrified. Suddenly, although she could see nothing,
she felt the Moth's wheels touch the ground. She
throttled down, trying to steer, while the machine
swayed and bumped over the invisible ground. But it
didn't turn over, it didn't hit anything, and in the end
it stopped. Amy climbed out and pulled the Moth
around to face into the wind but the force of the wind
started to push the little aircraft backwards. She
dragged luggage out of the front cockpit to act as
chocks behind the wheels, and struggled in the stinging, blinding sand to fasten a cover over the engine.
Then, feeling her way along the length of the aircraft,
she sat on the tail trying to weight it down, huddled
with her back to the storm. Where was she? What—or
who—was out there where she couldn't see? Dogs
began barking. Terrified, she grabbed her revolver.
Desert dogs could rip a body to pieces, she'd heard
those stories.

After three hours the wind died down enough
to give some visibility. Amy raced around the Moth
stuffing everything back in the cockpit, dropping tools
in the sand, desperate in case she lost her chance and

the duststorm closed in again. Anything to get back up in the air. She uncovered the engine, swung the propeller—luck was with her and the engine started—and took off in the direction she thought she would find Baghdad, arriving fairly soon afterwards. One of Amy's skills was an unerring sense of direction. As she landed at the Imperial Airways aerodrome the aircraft swung round and sank down on one wing. An undercarriage strut had sheared in two, probably strained during the landing in the desert. The damage could not be repaired and there were no spare parts in Baghdad. The end of the fourth day, and it seemed to be all over.

But the RAF produced 10 mechanics who worked through the night at the nearby RAF hangars to make her a new strut. The engine was overhauled and everything cleaned up. "Sporting help," said Amy. "I couldn't have managed without it."

By Karachi Amy Johnson had clipped two days off Hinkler's time. The press began to take notice and suddenly she was Amy Johnson, the "Lone Girl Flyer", the "British Girl Lindbergh". She was big news. Every day she landed out of the sky and the story of that day's flying was whisked up and sent by cable to be turned into exciting copy for the world's newspapers. The flight was always on the knife-edge between success and failure. One bad landing too many, an unlucky fault in the engine, and the attempt would be finished. She was pushing herself punishingly: three hours' work on the engine often by torchlight, after a day's flying, on average three hours' sleep a night.

Coming into Rangoon in torrential rain, petrol failing, daylight failing, she could not find anything which looked like the racecourse on which she was supposed to land. Amy saw an open space with a building which she thought must be the racecourse, only to come down and realise too late that the space was far too small; she ended up in a ditch, *Jason* damaged, herself in tears. The building turned out to be a government technical institute and she had landed on the playing field. The rain poured down, the ground was sticky mud, insects bit, and no-one knew anything about aeroplanes. *Jason* had a badly damaged wing, broken propeller, ripped tyre and a broken undercarriage strut—again. They lifted the aircraft out of the ditch and carried it to some distant trees for shelter. Amy went to bed exhausted.

Work began next morning. The propeller was replaced by the spare, and Amy got the mud out of the engine and serviced it. Students at the college welded a new strut, made bolts, straightened bent metal. An English forestry inspector glued the bits of broken wing ribs together and made some more. A shop in Rangoon had used war-surplus aeroplane linen to make men's shirts. About 20 shirts were torn into strips and Rangoon women pieced them together for wing-covering. There was not enough dope left to tighten and strengthen the fabric so a local chemist tried to work out the ingredients by smelling the little bit Amy had left over, and mixed up something which was adequate.

Two full days had been lost. Amy's time was now equal with Hinkler's. But ill luck and appalling weather continued and gradually she slipped behind in her schedule. This year the monsoon broke early and she struck the worst opening storms. Thick clouds and rain delayed her flight over the mountains to Bangkok. Flying on south the rain was so heavy, visibility so poor, she gave up and landed at Singora, where the Smiths had also landed after agonising hours of flying through torrential rain. At least she could overhaul the engine in daylight.

The aerodrome surface was soft sand and the
Moth's wheels sank in too deep for taxiing. Amy
decided she must take off along a nearby road. Next
morning she was appalled to find the road lined with
people—happy, picnicking, festive people—children
in front, lines of monks in saffron robes, chattering
women, curious men. Two human hedges come to see
an aeroplane, unaware of any danger. Amy tried to get
the people to move back a little. The horror of
swerving! The road was uncomfortably short for a safe
take-off and ended in houses and tall trees. Amy could
only steer by looking over one side, because it was
impossible to see straight ahead from the cockpit of
the Gipsy Moth. She shouted and gesticulated, and
little by little the people moved back. Heart in her
mouth, Amy started the engine and sped forward. She
looked over the side, got a spurt of petrol in her eyes,
half-blinding her, rushed on between the children, the
staring amazed faces, the yellows, pinks and greens, in
the steaming heat—lifted *Jason*'s nose, cleared the
trees and was away. "My relief to be in the air was
unspeakable."

Flying at last over the Timor Sea, $19\frac{1}{2}$ days
since leaving England and well behind Hinkler's time,
Amy, like other pilots, longed to see Australia. She
counted as far as she could in French and German.
She recited all the nursery rhymes and poems she
could remember. The much-repaired *Jason* flew on, it
seemed, unbearably slowly, rips in the wing's fabric
held together by pink sticking plaster, the engine
occasionally spluttering. The petrol at the last stop
had been lying around in huge rusty casks and needed
double filtering, and Amy was worried that a little
piece of rust might still have got through.

Then, in the distance, a dark cloud on the
horizon slowly turned into a shape, which became an
island, Melville Island, and she knew she was on

course, and that Darwin lay ahead. Her face and hands were burnt brick-red. She had discarded her heavy flying suit for a pair of men's khaki shorts and a drill jacket. She was oil-stained, and weary almost beyond belief. But she had done it.

Amy landed in Australia on Saturday 24 May 1930 to a tumultuous, overwhelming welcome. Utterly exhausted, the 26-year-old pilot was caught up in the first stages of a triumphal tour around Australia. Flying down the usual route from Darwin, she was escorted by aircraft chartered by newspapers and oil companies. One was piloted by C. W. A. Scott, soon to enter the long-distance flying stakes. Stopping briefly to refuel in Cloncurry she begged for time to visit the town quickly, to wash and rest. She was still feeling very tired and her period had begun. "She ought to be used to feminine problems by now—that's her business. Ours is to be on time at each appointment and we are leaving as soon as she's refuelled," was the only reply, and the cavalcade went on, relentlessly, according to a schedule already drawn up. Flying into Brisbane two days later, on Thursday, Amy Johnson crashed and *Jason* was damaged beyond immediate use.

Amy Johnson was learning what it meant to be a celebrity, to be a kind of public property. People just wanted to see her. She was mobbed, and paraded, put on show, expected to make speeches, go to balls, ride in cavalcades, open charity events—appear as often as possible to as many people as possible. She was given expensive gifts: opal and diamond jewellery, a watch, cigarette case and boomerang all of gold, clothes, tennis racquets, loving cups. Telegrams and cables kept arriving in Australia. The King and Queen sent their congratulations on her "... wonderful and courageous achievement". So did the British Prime

Minister. Louis Blériot, who in 1909 had been the first to fly an aeroplane across the Channel, cabled one word: "Bravo!"

Back home in England the public were waiting to claim her. Newspapers had vied for her story and time. She was portrayed as young and pretty, brave and daring, just an ordinary girl from Yorkshire, a typist, yet now she was world-famous. She was in fact a woman with a university degree plus pilot and engineering qualifications. The public hero-worshipped her. They were intensely proud of her. "Amy, wonderful Amy," went the words of a hit song,

"How can you blame me for loving you?
Since you've won the praise of ev'ry nation,
You have filled my heart with admiration . . ."

Amy had originally intended making the return trip from Australia to England in her Gipsy Moth. Now, still weary with the strain of the flight and the triumphal tour, she left for England the only way possible, by sea, picking up the Imperial Airways air route in Egypt. Huge crowds, estimated at a million people, lined the roads from Croydon Aerodrome into London on an August Bank Holiday Monday, to catch a glimpse of her as she was driven by.

Hinkler's time still stood. The England–Australia air route beckoned the seekers after records and four more aircraft set out in September and October 1930. Charles Kingsford Smith left last in a new Avro Avian *Southern Cross Junior*. Like Bert Hinkler, Kingsford Smith had been prevented from entering in the 1919 Air Race and the unfinished business stuck in his ambition. Now he was a world-famous long-distance aviator and he would fly the route faster than anyone: "Whatever record was set up, I was determined to beat it." His aircraft could fly high and fast, and extra fuel tanks gave it a range of around 2700 kilometres (1700 miles). Aeroplane engines were becoming much more reliable. And the aerodromes along the route were improving. Even then, when Kingsford Smith left England on 9 October, one of the other aircraft in the unofficial race had already broken down in Rangoon.

Like Amy's Gipsy Moth, Kingsford Smith's Avro was equipped as a self-contained unit. It carried the usual spare parts and spare propeller, emergency rations of beef, malt, chocolate and fresh water, a revolver and ammunition, and a special petrol-filling device of jointed piping, with funnels and chamois-leather strainers, to save time on stopovers.

Flying over the French coast Kingsford Smith made a detour to Beauvais to pay his last respects to dead friends. In the grey dawn the metal skeleton of Britain's great hope, the airship R101, in which so much had been invested, lay sprawled along the ground. The maiden flight to India, launched with so much celebration five days ago, had ended here in the fire and death of a crash. Good friends to aviation had been killed, including the Director of Civil Aviation, Sir Sefton Brancker, and the Secretary of State for Air, Lord Thomson. Brancker, who had made the round trip to India so courageously with Cobham in 1924–5 had not believed the airship ready, or proved fit, but Thomson had insisted the flight should take place. Just before leaving, Brancker had sent flowers to Amy Johnson, who was in hospital suffering from nervous exhaustion after too heavy a dose of publicity.

The only way to break Hinkler's time to Australia was by flying longer stages and making fewer stops. Kingsford Smith managed the same distance as Hinkler on the first day, London to Rome. Then he swung over to Athens, across to a French Air Force landing ground at Aleppo in Turkey, on down the Persian Gulf to the Imperial Airways base at Bushire, followed by a long non-stop stage of 1801 kilometres (1119 miles) to Karachi, arriving in India in five days. The crew of another aeroplane in the unofficial race met him here in Karachi and admitted defeat. One other aircraft without the range or quite the speed of the Avro was still ahead, flown by a determined rival, Flight-Lieutenant C. W. Hill, who was tackling night flying in his attempt to keep in front.

On before dawn to Allahabad; 12 hours' non-stop flying to Rangoon where it was permissible to land on the racecourse because it wasn't Saturday; a weary 14 hours to Singapore, the longest stage, 2013 kilometres (1251 miles); then, after slight repairs to the Avro by RAF mechanics, on to land at the Royal Dutch Airline aerodrome at Surabaya. That evening Kingsford Smith sat on the cool verandah of an English banker's bungalow wearing his host's pyjamas and dressing-gown, sipping iced lime squash. The roaring engine noise, the constant strain of concentrating, the long hours cramped in the cockpit—all were briefly forgotten in the joy of deep cushions and the peace of resting. Only the previous evening Hill had sat in the same chair, tired almost to the point of collapse but still determined to stay ahead. Hill knew that if he beat Hinkler's record he would hold it for about 24 hours because Kingsford Smith's time would be better.

Kingsford Smith left stiff and weary at dawn to fly along the islands to the landing ground at Atambua in Timor, the last stop before Darwin. As he came down after the day's flying the setting sun glinted on something metal. A sad sunburnt figure in topee and shorts came towards him. It was Hill. Taking off that morning, a whole day ahead, but heavily loaded for the Timor Sea crossing, he had failed to come unstuck in time and crashed into a fence. "Poor chap! My heart bled for him," said Kingsford Smith, and tried to work out a way of including him on the last stage. One passenger equalled the weight of essential fuel tanks so it was impossible. Hill lent Kingsford Smith his collapsible rubber boat, much more comforting than the inflated tubes which were all Kingsford Smith had if he were forced down. He had never faced a long flight over ocean in a single-engined plane and did not relish it. "You imagine the engine is running not quite normally when over areas where a forced landing isn't possible," said Kingsford Smith. "You hear suspicious sounds." As he flew on and on he chainsmoked and tried not to think about the water below. At 1.05 p.m. he saw the tip of Bathurst Island and shouted for joy, and sang unheard into the roar of the engine. And at 1.50 in the afternoon of 19 October 1930 he landed at Fannie Bay, 11 years after the first Smiths, just under 10 days from England, more than 1600 kilometres (1000 miles) travelled on average each day. Only two years ago Hinkler's time of $15\frac{1}{2}$ days had astonished the world.

The flight had been rather unadventurous, even dull, said Kingsford Smith. Good. The last thing that should ever happen on a well-planned expedition is adventure. A record flight should be properly prepared beforehand, and accomplished without incident and to schedule. This is the secret of success, plus the capacity for monotonous endurance, and familiarity with local conditions.

Kingsford Smith was describing the preconditions for successful commercial aviation as well as for record-breaking. He did in fact believe that his record flights proved the feasibility of establishing regular air services over long-haul routes. The distances could be brought within manageable limits, they were not vast and unbridgeable.

The record flights did get the public to realise that long journeys could take place by air, they did open up the possibilities of new air routes, and familiarise people with the idea of long-haul travel. But in many ways they were counterproductive to the needs of commercial aviation. They made some aspects of flying look easier than they were. Record-breakers were generally allowed to behave as they needed to achieve their aims. They chose their own routes; they droned on through the skies and landed where and when they had to. Local maintenance facilities were made available to them. They used the ground mechanics and spare parts and hospitality of air force bases. Overnight stops were generally no difficulty—people were keen to entertain famous fliers. At the same time the problems showed how closely commercial flights would have to conform to local laws. Record-breaking aviators were on occasion refused permission to depart, given long medical examinations and injections, arrested, even imprisoned by various governments en route. And as always, the record-breakers flew protected from the reality of commercial aviation's need to carry a payload. By comparison most commercial aircraft appeared to sidle along at slow speeds over short stages.

Record-breaking flights were made with bravado and courage. In some ways the First World War pilot ethos was operating again—heroic, adventurous, death-defying. It is no coincidence that many of the record-breaking aviators were ex-war pilots. There was a kind of reckless daredevil quality, a determination to carry out an objective come what may. And the record-breaking hotted up, became almost a frenzy.

Successful pilots seemed to get caught up in it, hitting again and again at the same objectives.

It was a time of world economic depression; "I could get no work as a pilot. Why not try and beat Hinkler's time?" said Charles Chabot, one of the contestants in the unofficial England to Australia race in October 1930. Newspapers revelled in describing the record attempts. The Depression also meant that money was short for anyone who wanted to develop ideas in aeroplane design or equipment, or run aviation companies. Bert Hinkler built an aeroplane to his own design but failed to sell it, and he embarked on more outstanding pioneer flights. Amy Johnson's dream of a career in aviation seemed to turn into a career in record-breaking. Kingsford Smith's own commercial aviation company failed and he was back on the circuit. His record time from England to Australia made in 1930 held no magic and it was soon broken. Flights along the route hammered back and forth with little value except brief publicity for the pilot concerned. It seemed necessary to hold records for both ways now. During 1931, 1932 and 1933 record times were made, lost and forgotten in the latest attempts. The record-breakers were operating within their own criteria of hours and minutes, of physical and mental endurance, of short cuts and risk-taking. Aviators like C. W. A. Scott, Kingsford Smith and James Mollison began flying with almost no rests, flying at night, flying longer and longer stages. It was the only way to do the distance. Record-breaking, said Geoffrey de Havilland, the aeroplane designer, had become a highly dangerous farce. The England–Australia route had turned into an endurance test of the crudest, cruellest kind.

And in the end a risk did not come off, equipment failed, luck cut the other way. Crashes came. Death destroyed flier, machine and dreams. Bert Hinkler failed to arrive at any airport the first night out from England on a record attempt to Australia in January 1933. His body was found months later when spring melted the snows from the Italian mountainside where he had crashed.

Commercial aviation had to be free of images of heroics and death. Just as in the beginning commercial aviation had to work hard to separate itself from the ethos of First World War flying, now the establishment of successful services along the aerial highways of the world required images of safety, reliability, pleasure and comfort.

11

Experiments with Airmail

A SMALLISH MOUND OF MAILBAGS travelled from London along the Imperial Airways route to India in April 1931. In Karachi they were loaded into the five-year-old DH66 Hercules *City of Cairo* and despatched towards Australia in a much-planned England to Australia experimental airmail flight: 15,000 pieces of mail about to arrive at their destination in half the time taken by a ship.

Flying down the islands of the East Indies the Imperial Airways DH66 ran out of petrol after just over six hours in the air. The pilot searched desperately for a flat place to land and chose something that looked green and smooth. But the greenness was tall grass hiding jagged boulders and the Hercules crashed, a write-off, a short distance from Kupang, on the island of Timor.

Qantas had a contract with Imperial Airways to pick up the mailbags in Darwin and fly them along their central Queensland route to Brisbane. Here Kingsford Smith and Ulm's commercial airline company, Australian National Airways, would take over the mail and distribute it to the southern cities. But Qantas could do nothing about rescuing the mail

Charles Kingsford Smith (centre) and Scotty Allan (far right) are
farewelled by the Superintendent of Mails before departing in the
Southern Cross on the experimental airmail flight, April 1931
(Captain G. U. Allan)

stranded in Timor because they had no aircraft capable of crossing the Timor Sea. Kingsford Smith's company had and he leapt at the chance, flying the famous *Southern Cross* up to Kupang, picking up the mailbags from the disconsolate Imperial Airways pilots and shuttling them on to Darwin. There he handed them over to the waiting Qantas aeroplane, collected the outgoing mails and flew them up through the islands as far as Akyab in Burma. The only hitch was at Surabaya where the heavy *Southern Cross* got bogged in the wet muddy landing ground, and had to be dug out by Javanese soldiers and local Dutchmen.

At Akyab an Imperial Airways Hercules collected the bags—nearly double the number of items which had been flown into Australia—and sped them on to London, the first "All-the-way-by-Air" Mail. The mail had taken 24 days London to Brisbane, and 19 days for the reverse journey. The British government had arranged for two experimental airmail flights, leaving London three weeks apart on 4 April and 25 April, so *Southern Cross* waited in Akyab to collect the second consignment of mailbags from an Imperial Airways aircraft and fly them on to Darwin where Qantas again took over with their DH61. The second load of Australian mail left from Darwin in an Imperial Airways aircraft. The British had managed to buy a Hercules in Australia which flew successfully through to meet the scheduled service in Karachi. The times were better—18 days and 16 days—but the disastrous crash in Timor tarnished the whole exercise.

In the meantime the Dutch airline company KLM, which was running a regular weekly service between Amsterdam and Batavia, organised a special

"Holland—Australia" airmail flight arriving without hitches at Wyndham on the north-west coast and linking up with Western Australian Airways.

Posting a letter in Australia for England and waiting for a reply had always been a tedious business. The Englishmen who first came to live in Australia had to wait two to three years while sailing ships worked across the oceans. Now in the early 1930s the reply to a letter took at least two months. The delay was bad for business and frustrating. Lifting letters by aeroplane would speed things up wonderfully, and the need for airmail was a sufficient reason, many thought, to develop an air route, fast. Christmas was a time when people separated from their family and friends by half the world felt particularly isolated. When Kingsford Smith and Ulm announced they would send a special all-Australian airmail to England for Christmas 1931, the response was enormous. The propaganda value was high: Kingsford Smith and Ulm reckoned the airmail bonanza would demonstrate how efficiently and reliably their airline company could fly the long-haul route. The company had been forced to close down their non-subsidised Australian routes in July 1931. The Christmas airmail would be flown in one of the company's fleet of Avro Xs, a single-wing three-engined Fokker made under licence in England. Australian government regulations forbad the purchase of non-British aircraft but the licensing agreement got around the regulations.

The original announcement of the Christmas flight offered places to passengers but so much mail was piling up there was only weight spare for one, an important piece of human freight. Colonel Horace Brinsmead, Director of Civil Aviation, wanted to travel to England to discuss the question of setting up a

Scotty Allan, pilot of *Southern Sun* VH-UNA in the first
all-Australian airmail flight, and Charles Kingsford Smith
(right), November 1931 (Qantas Collection)

regular England–Australia airmail service. A second
passenger, very irate, had to be left behind.

The heavily laden Avro X *Southern Sun* left
Sydney on 20 November 1931. Six days later it
crashed on take-off in Malaya at Alor Star, north of
Penang. The landing ground was under water, one
engine was malfunctioning and the aircraft failed to
drag free. Pilot "Scotty" Allan jumped a dyke and
belly-flopped into a paddy field, wrecking the aircraft
but fortunately injuring no-one. As soon as Charles
Kingsford Smith heard of the crash in Sydney he set
out in another Avro X *Southern Star* to collect the mail
and relay it on to London. The monsoon was flinging
the usual dense rain, lightning and heavy cloud over
an area from Burma to Darwin. Flying into Darwin in
poor visibility, Kingsford Smith struck a telegraph
post and tore wing fabric, dented the propeller and
damaged a cylinder. Colonel Brinsmead waiting at
Alor Star heard of the crash and decided he must
hurry on to England via one of the regular KLM
services. The Dutch aeroplane crashed taking off from
Bangkok, killing five, and Brinsmead was so severely
hurt he died from his injuries within three years.

After losing three days over repairs in Darwin
Kingsford Smith reached the stranded mail, collected
it and flew on with Scotty Allan. The route was
familiar now. He had done it once in July 1929 with
Southern Cross, made the record-breaking solo flight
along it in October 1930; travelled part way four times
in April–May this year bailing out Imperial Airways,
and had just flown the whole way in September–
October in a ghastly attempt to re-establish a new solo
Australia–England record, a flight dogged by engine
failure, forced landings and a desperate illness in
which he vomited, blacked out and came close to
disaster. It had ended in the fiasco of imprisonment by

the Turks. Now it was December and here he was
doing it again.

The landing ground at Calcutta was heavy with
mud and water and *Southern Star* bogged badly and
had to be dug out by everyone available. They were
flying from monsoon rain straight into a European
winter. Wicked snowstorms over the Apennines were
followed by such dense fog at Lyon in France that
they couldn't see the length of their aeroplane. How
far did the fog extend? No weather forecasts were
available. When the fog cleared a little they took off
from Lyon hoping to get above the murk, but they
never did, so they steered a compass course for
England, occasionally glimpsing the dim shape of
trees and nothing else until suddenly the water of the
Channel was heaving close below, and the fog was still
thick all around. Allan, who was piloting, conferred
with Kingsford Smith and both men decided they
must risk landing on the nearest beach. Allan brought
the big three-engined aircraft down onto firm sand by
the edge of the sea, and taxied along until a hotel
appeared. They turned at right angles up the beach,
and slept the night at the Hôtel Bristol, Le Touquet.
Next morning the fog had lifted and the town turned
out to see them take off. Their arrival at Croydon on
16 December created much publicity for the 45,288
letters and packets flown all the way from Australia
for an English Christmas.

Kingsford Smith offered to take a New Year
mail back to Australia. The English weather was
terrible with snowstorms and bitter cold. "It was
enough to kill a sun-loving Australian and I could
never get warm," said Kingsford Smith. The Avro had
been sent to the aircraft works for inspection and
reconditioning. On New Year's Eve it was due to be
flown back to Croydon ready for take-off. There were

delays leaving the factory and pilot Allan realised he
could not make Croydon before dark.

The factory phoned the airport to tell them to
turn on their lights for the approaching aircraft.
Arriving over London, Allan found himself in fog and
poor visibility. He flew by dead reckoning to where
Croydon ought to be but there were no lights to guide
him down. He flew backwards and forwards looking
for landmarks and re-approaching where he thought
Croydon was, but still no lights. The co-pilot was a
Londoner but he was just as lost. Once Allan glimpsed
a railway station and came down low to read its name:
Pittswood. Where is that? Never heard of it. No
Pittswood on any map. In fact it was a new station
only opened that week. By now fuel was running low
so they flew by dead reckoning into the comparative
flatness of Kent and began circling, searching down
into the darkness for an area with no lights which
would minimise crashing onto buildings. "We didn't
want to land in somebody's cottage." A choice had to
be made. They had to come down onto a particular
piece of land in this crowded part of England, on a
cold New Year's night. Allan chose, and began to bring
the aircraft lower, lower. Trees ahead, silhouetted
against the gloom. He hauled *Southern Star* over the
branching shapes and landed in a field, bumping
along, an extraordinary and successful touchdown
until suddenly the big machine ploughed into apple
trees, knocking over 25, breaking propellers, damaging the undercarriage and forcing the wings out of
alignment.

The repairs were carried out quickly but gales
delayed departure until 7 January, when Kingsford
Smith and Allan at last took off with over 70,000
pieces of mail. Despite the winter weather and the
monsoons the journey was uneventful until they

reached the last stop in the East Indies, Kupang in
Timor. Rain was sheeting down, but they took off
from the sodden airfield only to be driven back by the
rain—they could not see through the grey waterfalls of
water, and only found the landing ground again with
great difficulty, touching down gingerly onto the
waterlogged surface. The aircraft was bogged to the
axles. Everything had to be unloaded in the pouring
rain and mucky mud and 200 natives hauled and
shoved at the heavy machine to get it free. "Kupang
must be the muddiest place in the world," said
Kingsford Smith, "with Alor Star a close second." The
two pilots left their personal luggage and some spare
parts behind to lighten the load, and next day they got
away, reaching Darwin on 19 January 1932.

The Christmas airmail flight had cost one
wrecked Avro X, two crashes to a second Avro X, plus
sundry boggings and forced landings, and coin-
cidentally the near death of the Director of Civil
Aviation. "We had demonstrated," said Charles
Kingsford Smith with some bravado, "despite accidents, floods, fogs, wretched aerodromes and poor
ground-organisation, that the Empire airmail was a
practical possibility."

The Dutch had been demonstrating the equivalent for several years, to British annoyance. KLM,
under their founder Albert Plesman, ran a regular
once-weekly all-the-year-round service from Amsterdam to Batavia, the capital of the Dutch East
Indies, carrying both passengers and mail. The need
was obvious, said Plesman, for an "express service"
between Europe and the Far East. The argument
about whether letters or people should be the payload,
whether the mail should have priority, was irrelevant.
"There is no reason why a passenger should travel less
quickly than a letter"—irritating and irrefutable logic

The KLM Fokker XVIII flew the Amsterdam–Batavia route in 9 or 10 days, carrying passengers and mail (KLM)

for Imperial Airways whose aircraft could manage
both, but slowly and only part-way. In 1932 Imperial
Airways were taking five and a half days to get to the
edge of India using three different aircraft, the French
and Italian railways, and sundry motor launches,
motorcars and coaches. A three-engined KLM Fokker
XVIII monoplane carried a payload of up to four
passengers and 500 kilograms (1100 pounds) of mail
along the 14,500-kilometre (9000-mile) route, Amsterdam to Batavia, in 9 or 10 days depending on
whether it was winter or summer in Europe.

The Dutch did not believe in different aircraft
for each section of the route. The same aircraft made
the return journey out to the Far East and back with
no change of crew, exactly like a ship. They did
without relief crews along the route and a fleet of only
six aircraft operated the whole service. The strain—
physical and mental—on the crew was heavy, but
Plesman believed it was acceptable. The flight to
Batavia was followed by nearly two weeks' rest in the
islands, another week's holiday after the return trip to
Holland, then crews did seven weeks on scheduled
routes within Europe. Each crew therefore made four
return trips to the East Indies a year. Crew members
suffered most commonly from sunstroke, heatstroke,
malaria and intestinal troubles. Each day's flying
along the route lasted eight to nine hours, with up to
two intermediate refuelling stops, from just before
sunrise to one hour before sunset. The commander
and first officer alternated two hours on, two hours off
at the wheel. The third crew member was an engineer
who serviced the Fokker each night after landing, and
serviced passengers during the day with simple steward duties. The fourth crew member was a trained
wireless operator who kept in contact with radio
stations and used the new direction-finding devices for

navigating. Since there were no KLM staff or ground mechanics along the route he also helped the engineer service the aircraft. The radio was useful for informing aerodromes of expected time of arrival and warning agents about the number of passengers to expect. After landing at Batavia details of the flight were sent back to headquarters in Amsterdam by radio: state of engines, instruments, landing grounds, health of the crew, weather encountered, fuel used and quantities of mail and passengers. The three Pratt and Whitney "Wasp" engines of 420 horsepower were overhauled after two round trips, or 290 hours of flying. Each Fokker was equipped for emergency landings in desert or jungle. Mosquito nets were stored on board, emergency tins of water and food, a distilling machine, wound dressings, a medicine chest and revolvers. Some spare parts and tools were necessary for en route servicing, and 10 large Thermos flasks full of food were packed each day for inflight catering.

The Dutch had found that the route threw fogs and ice at the aircraft, sandstorms and duststorms, monsoon rain and thunder clouds, but never all at once. Political difficulties had wasted more of the company's energy than any technical problems. But a route had been achieved giving pleasant overnight stops where passengers and crew could wash, eat and sleep, and the plane be refuelled. Meals and accommodation were included in the cost of a ticket and the commander paid for anything extra so passengers did not need to change currency, a bill being presented at the end.

The pilots were considered by KLM to have a most responsible job. They had to be trained airmen, but also linguists, administrators, be commercially knowledgeable, tactful in handling passengers, yet keep strict discipline on board. "Aeroplanes are becoming more complex," commented Plesman, "with new instruments to help with flying in fog or darkness being added to the cockpit. The number of handles, knobs and switches increases; soon our already busy pilots will need switchboards and instrument boards. They have large numbers of papers to deal with: maps and sea-charts, sketches and descriptions of aerodromes and places where forced landings can be made, tables giving times of sunrise and sunset, data about the influence of height above sea-level and air temperature on take-off performance, lists about what one is not allowed to take into countries along the route."

In 1933 Plesman had a new aeroplane in construction, the Fokker XX, able to fly even faster with a greater range than his existing aircraft. But in the future, Plesman reckoned, when the journey was down to four days, passengers would have to get up at 2 a.m. each day and fly, literally, from bed to bed.

Imperial Airways argued that comparisons with the Dutch were not fair. The British were obliged to pick up and deliver mail and passengers all along their route. the Dutch were flying end to end with intermediate stops only to refuel and rest. Most of the 446 passengers carried by KLM and their subsidiary. KNILM, in 1932 on the Amsterdam—Batavia route travelled the whole way. The Dutch Post Office also paid a subsidy for a set weight of mail regardless of how much was carried. The British Post Office did this for ships but not aeroplanes. paying only for what was sent by air, so KLM had a regular income denied to Imperial Airways. The truth was that Albert Plesman ran a tight, modern, well-planned, thrifty organisation, getting longer hours and faster turnarounds from crews and machines. And the Fokkers were excellent, well-proven aeroplanes. The existence of the efficient

Dutch air route—the world's longest regular airmail and passenger service—was a constant irritant to the British. Too many people asked why Imperial Airways ran leisurely schedules compared to KLM's apparently speedy service. And KLM constantly offered to fly on to Australia. "Free trade of the air", Plesman called it, knowing he held the advantages. The offers at least spurred the British and Australian governments on to sorting through the problems preventing a commercial air route finally spanning the whole distance, England through to Australia.

12

Voyage of the *Astraea*

QANTAS APPEARED TO BE WELL PLACED to carry the overseas mails. Darwin was the obvious point of entry on the north coast, and Qantas organised the greatest part of the route south through the sparsely inhabited outback country. The decision back in 1920 by two young returned airmen to try to service isolated Queensland railhead towns by aeroplane had far-reaching implications. Qantas was now a reliable airline run prudently and conscientiously by Hudson Fysh, with a strong commitment to safety. But they were small—"bushies" to other city-based operators who desperately wanted the Australian government contract to carry the overseas mails. Fysh knew that Qantas must be included in the running of the chosen route; otherwise they would be elbowed out, a casualty after the years of effort.

No-one knew what would be the shape or composition of the final pieces of jigsaw needed to complete the England–Australia route. It had been talked about for so long and was always expected to happen some time in the future. Did Imperial Airways intend to fly all the way to Australia and hand over at the front door? Would Australians create an overseas company, venture beyond national airspace, to link up with Imperial Airways somewhere along the route? Would aeroplanes carry mail only, or passengers as well? Fysh knew that Qantas did not have the resources to set up an air route beyond Australia. Partnership with other Australian companies would risk his, and Qantas', submergence. Partnership between Imperial Airways, or even KLM, and an Australian company was sought by no-one, at least in the beginning.

Stalling tactics, fast footwork, heavy politicking, meetings, squabbles and correspondence filled the months with no solution being created. But everyone got on with secret negotiations. Imperial Airways and Qantas began to draw towards some form of partnership, although the form it would take wavered and swelled into various shapes as letters were exchanged and British officials conferred in Australia and government pressure seemed to favour one aspect rather than another. Compromise waited on understanding the shifting reality. Private and opposing negotiations were going on even within the Qantas board, the Chairman preferring an all-Australian solution with Ulm and Kingsford Smith's company dominating, Fysh pursuing the British connection. Early in 1933 Fysh's victory became public. Imperial Airways and Qantas agreed to form a new company, 50/50, to operate a service between Brisbane and Singapore, and the company was to have an "Australian atmosphere".

Fysh's Australian opponents, in particular Ulm and Kingsford Smith, and Brearley of Western Australian Airways, were bitterly angry. "We trusted Qantas because it was run by Hudson Fysh," said Imperial Airways' management. Fysh is an Imperial Airways puppet, said his enemies in Australia. But Qantas' future had been guaranteed: as long, that is, as the new partnership won the Australian government contract, which was put out to tender. Only the "British" (which included Australians) could tender, which cut out KLM, and all aeroplanes and engines used on any section of the new route had to be manufactured in the British Empire.

Fysh wanted the de Havilland Company, based on the northern edge of London, to build a new four-engined plane for the Brisbane–Singapore route. Qantas had been using DH aircraft for years and the company had facilities in Australia. Fysh reckoned that the Australian government at the end of the Depression would not be interested in a large expensive aircraft. He envisaged a smallish economical machine, an improvement on existing British aircraft, which could travel at 217 kilometres per hour (135 miles per hour) and be able to fly 970 kilometres (600 miles) against a 64 kilometre per hour (40 mile per hour) headwind. The ability to function on two out of the four engines would guarantee safety on the dreaded Timor Sea crossing. The England–Australia route would be the longest commercial air service in the world, and the Timor Sea—832 kilometres (517 miles)—would involve the longest over-sea journey of any commercial airline service in the world.

While negotiations were going on about which aircraft to use, Imperial Airways decided on a persuasive gesture. One of their large new four-engined AW XV Atalanta Class monoplanes, designed by Armstrong Whitworth for service on the Empire routes in India and South Africa, should fly to Australia on a goodwill route-proving flag-waving exercise. *Astraea* left England at the end of May 1933. Special flights would be offered to local dignitaries along the route with much ceremony and demonstration of British aviation pro-

Imperial Airways' AW XV Atalanta Class *Astraea* arriving in Brisbane on 23 June 1933 (Qantas Collection)

wess. In particular *Astraea* would inaugurate Imperial
Airways' extension to the route across India from
Karachi to Calcutta. At the appointed time guests were
seated in the luxurious 17-seat cabin, while British
officials and influential Indians watched, surrounded
by military pomp. Nothing happened. The engines
would not start. Four hours later they still would not
start. The fiasco was capped by another when *Astraea*
failed to make the Timor Sea crossing, and force-
landed out of petrol on Bathurst Island at an emergency landing ground hacked from the bush only weeks
before by the Aborigines at a Roman Catholic mission
station. The mission lugger made a 30-hour journey
into Darwin to fetch more fuel and critical Australians
mocked the British failure.

   Astraea toured Australian cities to a mixed
reception and departed for India in July, with Hudson
Fysh on board as one of the first passengers ever to fly
from Australia to England. To Fysh the trip was
magic. He hadn't been abroad since he sailed to the
war, a 19-year-old soldier in 1914. Now he was
actually flying out the top end of Australia and
immediately he was experiencing the glamorous
East—cloud-wreathed and jungle-clad volcanic
mountains, flooded paddy fields, intensive agriculture,
native huts glimpsed amongst the trees, the beat of
drums, the challenge of foreign currency. It was heady
stuff for Fysh. He had been building up a small airline
for 12 years, he had survived the early period of flying
while contemporaries had been killed, he was becoming an influential figure in Australia, but he hadn't
really travelled.

   The first night out from Darwin was as romantic as anyone would wish for. An unspoilt tropical
island with a total white population of five, and a

native-run rest house built of rushes and thatch up in the hills at Selong; dinner on the verandah of tough little fowls, omelettes and bananas, while moonlight spilled in patches through giant trees and lizards chirped in the roof. Dinner was very late because the fowls had escaped when the cook tried to catch them. He had to wait until they settled down to roost. Even sleeping was different. The rest house had only three large beds, so the six men from the *Astraea* slept in pairs, each separated by a hard bolster known as a "Dutch wife". The day had been long, eight hours in the air and 1682 kilometres (1045 miles) travelled. There had been one refuelling at Kupang, the landing ground on the island of Timor, then on up the chain of islands to this small volcanic island of Lombok.

The next evening an orchestra played while Fysh dined and danced with other guests in the luxury Hôtel des Indes, Batavia. *Astraea* had flown for hours up the long island of Java with its population six times that of Australia, and landed twice, at Surabaya and now Batavia, at excellent well-equipped airports used by KLM and its subsidiary KNILM. On the following morning a short flight over the equator and in past the steamers, junks and bumboats of Singapore's busy harbour to land at the RAF military aerodrome. A drive through rubber plantations and native villages to bed at the famous Raffles Hotel. "Each day had turned a new leaf of adventure ... all from the comfortable lounge seat in the *Astraea*," enthused Fysh. He hadn't even experienced the headaches and deafness usual with flying. He had finished each day feeling clean, almost fresh. But the flight on to Calcutta through the belt of vicious monsoon weather ahead would surely test the aircraft.

Like all airmen, Fysh almost subconsciously scanned the ground below for possible landing places. All the way up from Darwin there seemed to be nowhere to make a forced landing. Now, flying north from Singapore, the world looked inundated. Where swamps or flooded paddy fields finished, intensive cultivation or heavily timbered hills took over. Alor Star, where Kingsford Smith's Christmas airmail flight had come to grief two and a half years ago, was surrounded by water, and muddy pools on the surface of the aerodrome reflected a grey waterlogged sky. At Bangkok sheets of water sprayed up covering *Astraea*'s windows as they landed. Next day they must tackle the high, minimally mapped mountains between Bangkok and Rangoon, where Ross and Keith Smith back in 1919 had flown so perilously, through dense grey cloud. *Astraea* met the same kind of murky clouds covering all sign of land beneath or mountains ahead, but the cockpit was equipped with blind-flying instruments so the dangerous conditions could be dealt with.

The weather reports were so bad in Rangoon Fysh and his British friends stayed an extra day and went to the races, the "Second Monsoon Meeting". A rather awkward aerodrome had been built on the slope of a hill at Rangoon, leaving the racecourse free from landing aeroplanes. Hundreds of big wooden fans spun in the grandstands and tea-rooms and private boxes, moving the heavy air. Burmese beauties walked in their finery on carefully tended lawns amongst shrubs and trees of botanic gardens splendour.

A less powerful or well-equipped aircraft would not have attempted the next day's flight to Calcutta. Storms rocked *Astraea* as it flew through heavily turbulent air, drenching rain darkened the cabin, and water penetrated the structure and sloshed around on the floor. Dum Dum aerodrome at Calcutta had to be located by the new direction-finding equipment.

Calcutta was soaking. The rain fell incessantly all next day and the one after when *Astraea*, now part of the regular Calcutta–Karachi service, took off, water thrashing past the windows like a bow wave. The route across India took just over one day, with stops for mail and passengers.

In Karachi Fysh changed over to the largest aeroplane he had ever seen, the 24-seat HP42 Hannibal. "Can this huge machine, with passenger cabins alone over 50 feet [16 metres] long, take the air?" Flying was even more comfortable and slightly quieter than in *Astraea*. The tropics were behind them now, the deserts lay ahead with summer at its height, and London was six days away. Barren hills, sandy plains, lonely, lonely country passed below while passengers ate their meals served from the stewards' efficient pantry, and read magazines. In a way Fysh was reminded of the outback Qantas route. The plane came down to refuel at isolated communities and transported odds and ends of freight—things needed in a hurry along the Gulf. Next day, flying towards Basra, a heavy sandstorm hit them, great yellow voluminous clouds blotting out the ground in minutes.

Basra itself, on the boundary between Iraq and Persia, with big oil refineries rising in the distance, was like an oven blasting with hot air. It more than equalled a heatwave day at Longreach. The night was spent at Baghdad and Fysh thought in wonder about his journey. The night before he had slept in a fort guarded by Arab sentries, the night before that in the luxurious hotel of the Maharajah of Jodhpur. The night before that in the steamy heat and monsoon rain of Calcutta where you could stumble over sleeping

Indians on the footpath in front of the Great Eastern
Hotel, or even in the hotel billiards room, and sacred
bulls stood where they wished and could not be
moved. Tonight he bought a drink with the sixth
currency since leaving Australia. Unable to miss any
opportunity, he toured Baghdad by taxi then got up at
a quarter to three for the next day's flight, after less
than two hours' sleep, but what did it matter? Three
and a half hours' flying brought them to breakfast at
the desert fort of Rutbah Wells, then on over the
enormous loneliness of the Syrian desert to land for
lunch in Gaza at a small aerodrome with a patchy
unreliable surface. Fysh felt a sense of real shock.
Sixteen years ago he had been fighting here. The
trenches he remembered so well could still be plainly
seen from the air. The aerodrome was still littered with
fragments of high-explosive shells. But this was a long
day and they had to get on to Cairo, with an evening
train still to catch to the port of Alexandria.

Early in the morning Hudson Fysh was rowed
out to his first flying boat, the four-engined Short
Kent Class *Satyrus*, for the Mediterranean crossing.
They flew low over the water and Fysh sat back in an
upholstered chair behind a table with a tablecloth and
vase of flowers, imagining he was in a large private
yacht. Refuelling in Crete, some of the passengers
changed into bathing clothes and swam off the side of
the aircraft. Then on to the excitement of a first view
of Athens, so close yet no time for visiting, then up
over Greek islands and along magnificent coastline to
Italy. Fysh decided that only the beaches of New South
Wales were more beautiful. The Italy of Mussolini
forbad any photographs of naval installations at the
port of Brindisi, the flying boat base, so all cameras
were placed in a sealed bag. Then just time for dinner
in Italy and off on the long train journey to Paris, a

Short S.17 Kent *Satyrus* G-ABFC flying across the
Mediterranean (RAF Museum, Hendon)

lurching, vibrating, dirty trip, Fysh thought, compared with air travel. Two nights and a day to cover a distance manageable in 12 to 14 hours by aeroplane. Arriving in Paris early in the morning of the second day a bus picked the London-bound passengers up from the station and took them to a hotel for coffee and rolls. Paris!—but so briefly. Another bus had them at the airport by 8.30 a.m., men in dark suits and coats, hats and scarves, women in fur-collared coats and smart shoes and pull-on felt cloches. You dressed in your best to fly in the HP42 from Paris to London. This HP42 was luxuriously appointed for the European routes with seats like roomy armchairs and tables for writing and dining.

Fysh filmed from the cabin window the wheels touching English soil at 11.15 on the morning of 24 July. He had left Longreach, central Queensland, 17 days ago. He felt as if the world in all its wonder had been dragged past his hungry eyes at an enormous rate. He had slept little. Had he been travelling by boat he would still be at Colombo, in India—but the new air service would have to be much faster still.

While in England Fysh negotiated the form of the partnership between Imperial Airways and Qantas and decided with Imperial Airways to inaugurate the new service with the as yet unbuilt 10-seater de Havilland four-engined aircraft, to be known as the DH86. He returned home to Australia via the United States, having travelled by air as many stages of his round-the-world trip as possible. The Atlantic Ocean, the Pacific Ocean and the Tasman Sea could still only be crossed by ship.

On 19 April 1934 the waiting was over and the Australian government announced that Imperial Airways and Qantas had won the right to run Australia's overseas air service with their new company, Qantas Empire Airways. QEA, registered on 18 January 1934

with Hudson Fysh as managing director, was owned
49 per cent by each company, with two per cent held
by an independent "umpire" adjudicating a fair and
balanced partnership should that aim ever slip. The
Australian government had decided that mails leaving
Australia should start their journey from the railway
station in a small inland New South Wales town called
Cootamundra. The Australian government was sticking to a long-held decision that subsidised air routes
must not duplicate existing railway lines. From Cootamundra the mail would be flown up to the Queensland
town of Charleville on the original Qantas route. The
contract for this spur line was awarded to a new
airline, Butler Air Transport, not QEA. Western Australian airmail would be carried from Perth up to
Katherine on the Overland Telegraph Line by another
new company, McRobertson Miller Aviation Company, where a train would take it the final 320
kilometres (200 miles) to Darwin. A new company
would carry the mail across Bass Strait from Hobart.
Kingsford Smith and Ulm, who got nothing, were dis-
appointed and angry.

By the end of the year Charles Ulm was dead,
having crashed into the sea short of Hawaii on an
attempted flight across the Pacific. Charles Kingsford
Smith died nearly a year later, disappearing close to
the Burmese coast trying to break, yet again, the
record time from England to Australia.

The Brisbane to Singapore route won by Qantas Empire Airways was one-third of the total England
to Australia route. Imperial Airways itself had only
just opened up the sections from Karachi through to
Singapore. The distances to be flown within Australia
by airline companies to distribute and collect airmail
were large. Establishing the final all-the-way service
had in fact taken much organising and would add
quite substantially to British Empire air routes.

13

Overseas Airmail Service

THE DE HAVILLAND AIRCRAFT COMPANY was very experienced in the traditional techniques of aircraft manufacture. De Havilland Moths were flown the world over; cheap, easy to manage, attractive small aircraft. The DH86 was their first four-engined machine, and they designed, built and tested it in the remarkably short time of four months because no more time was available. It got the necessary Certificate of Airworthiness the day before the tenders for the Australian route were due in. The DH86 was made of shaped woods, taut wires, with metal bracing out its fuselage and a covering of stretched and doped Irish linen. It was a biplane, considerably smaller and one-third the price of Armstrong Whitworth's *Astraea*, and roughly equivalent in size to the Smiths' 1919 Vickers Vimy. The DH86's four engines created 800 horsepower compared to the 720 horsepower of the Vimy's two engines. But the new aircraft could lift a payload of 10 passengers plus some mail and freight, and cruise in excess of specification at 233 kilometres per hour (145 miles per hour), with a range of 1230 kilometres (764 miles) in still air, enough to cope with the Timor Sea.

In most ways the DH86 was a superior stop-gap. Something had to be created to fit the Australian government's contract specifications, and fast. But there was an illogicality in the choice of a landplane. Imperial Airways had always insisted that flying boats must carry passengers across the open water of the Mediterranean, even though the change of machines at the water's edge slowed up the time taken to travel the route. The Dutch were happy to fly three-engined landplanes from Amsterdam to Batavia because they considered the route was largely over land. But beyond Batavia lay the most watery section and here Imperial Airways seemed content to support a landplane. No British flying boat in fact existed with sufficient range and payload to tackle the Timor Sea. In America Juan Trippe of Pan Am was commissioning long-range flying boats to fly the long stages of the proposed air route across the Pacific. No commercial aeroplanes could yet fly across the Atlantic Ocean—that most significant and lucrative of routes—and flying boats would probably be the answer there as well. But at the very time Fysh was deciding with Imperial Airways to order a new landplane from de Havilland, Imperial Airways was planning, secretly, a clean sweep of all their aircraft on the Empire routes. The scheme was first broached between top Imperial Airways officials travelling on a route-proving flight through to South Africa at the end of 1932. The officials decided to return to England by sea so they could discuss the implications during several weeks of shipboard life. The idea as finally agreed between Imperial Airways and the British government was for all first-class mail to be carried by air throughout the Empire, at a standard cheap rate subsidised by the government, on

a large fleet of new, specially designed, rugged flying
boats: a dramatic bold concept allowing British civil
aviation access to a consistent, technologically up-
dated aircraft. It would take several years to organise
this Empire Air Mail Scheme and nothing was made
public. Meanwhile plans went ahead to open the route
to Australia with a new untested landplane.

     The stop-gap qualities of the DH86 were even
more evident when it was compared with the revolutionary aircraft becoming available in America. Hudson Fysh saw the American breakthrough on his trip
to the States at the end of 1933. He was about to fly on
Boeing's new B247 on its night route across the
continent. "I felt depressed," said Fysh, "in a strange
land amongst new and risky things, and wondered
how I had ever been so foolish to book on such a
midnight horror, and doubted if I should ever again
see sunny Australia." But this B247 about which he
had heard scare reports in England did look all right
standing on the tarmac, a real aeroplane, and inside it
was roomy and comfortable and not noisy. They flew
all through the night in constant contact with radio
stations, with a revolving beacon marking the route
every four minutes (16 kilometres or 10 miles) and a
well-lit landing ground every eight minutes. The
United Airlines company had staff working all the 24
hours. When he was taken to see the new Douglas
DC-2 and the projected DC-3, Fysh was overwhelmed.
"All these high-speed machines here make everything
look out of date in England," he wrote privately to the
managing director of Imperial Airways. "[You must]
make your manufacturers realise cruising speeds of
160–200 miles per hour (260–320 kilometres per
hour) are safe, practical and essential too unless they
are to fall hopelessly behind." They had to move

quickly into the new techniques.

The two American planes, built by the companies of Bill Boeing and Donald Douglas, were revolutionary. With their sleek lines and swept-back wings, they incorporated the latest aerodynamic and structural knowledge. Here was the "modern" airliner. Both the DC-2 and the B247 were of all-metal "stressed-skin" construction. It had been worked out that if thin metal sheeting were stretched over a light but rigid metal framework, this outside skin of metal resisted stresses from all directions, and so could carry the bulk of a structural load, rather like an eggshell. Fuselages built on this principle were strong, weighed less and saved space. Their smooth streamlined exterior reduced drag. Designers worked out how to build strong, light, flexible wings, stretching the metal skin tightly over a series of small, box-like, rigid compartments, like a honeycomb. Douglas tested the extremely tough wing of the DC-2 by having a steamroller drive over it. There was not even a dent.

In 1928 an American engineer had discovered that if aircraft engines were encased in a streamlined cowling, leaving only the front and rear open for ventilation, much drag could be eliminated. And if the cowled engines were set into the wings themselves, mounted in pod-like housings known as "nacelles", they gained tremendously in efficiency. Both the DC-2 and B247 incorporated these advances. They had variable-pitch propellers, which allowed the achievement of a higher cruising speed, and retractable landing gear, which reduced drag, although it had to be cranked up and down by hand. The DC-2 had wing flaps—moveable sections on the wings which, when lowered, gave the aircraft more lift at take-off, and slowed it down to a safer speed when landing. The

B247 could carry 10 passengers and the DC-2 could
seat fourteen.

Hudson Fysh was thrilled by Douglas's guarantee that the DC-2 would cruise at 306 kilometres per
hour (190 miles per hour). He was impressed by the
simple practical way each 710-horsepower engine
could be changed in half an hour, the wonderful
attention to the detail of efficient servicing and
maintenance—everything was accessible and replaceable. The chairs were comfortable, and iced water was
always available in the cabin. "The Douglas is the
most ingenious, carefully thought-out high-speed aircraft ever put out and is a complete eye-opener." But
Fysh was an exceptionally loyal man. He had helped
to commission the DH86 and he would stick by it.
No-one else can offer a four-engined aircraft, he
maintained, with equivalent performance at such low
cost. But he did write to Imperial Airways' managing
director that the DH86 should be built of metal,
should have a retractable undercarriage and should be
able to achieve faster speeds. Fysh had seen the future
and he acknowledged it. But he stuck doggedly, even
fiercely, to the British reality, and he had no option.

Qantas pilot Lester Brain was sent to England
towards the end of 1934 to take delivery of the first
DH86 for Australia. Brain had never flown anything
except cap-and-goggles, open-cockpit, single-engined
aeroplanes. He had never sat in a closed cockpit, or
used more than one engine. Imperial Airways had
already taken delivery of one DH86, but Brain felt
unhappy with the design when he saw it at the de
Havilland works. The pilot sat alone in the narrow
nose. The first officer was supposed to sit behind in the
cabin and take over the controls by sidling in and
swapping over seats in mid-flight. That might be
manageable for Imperial Airways' European hops, but

on the long three and a half days' section between
Brisbane and Singapore, Brain was convinced pilots
would need dual controls. "Not actually possible,"
said de Havilland's; "changing the design will add
months to the delivery time, and there will be a
penalty in loss of speed." Brain felt an awkward new
boy from the colonies arguing against the top British
brass, not to mention de Havilland's experienced test
pilot. But he insisted, and with Hudson Fysh's backing, a snout-like nose was built on to the QEA DH86,
allowing dual controls, and it in fact flew faster than
the single-control version.

Brain wanted changes to the undercarriage
which he considered too lively and difficult to control,
he wanted flaps or airbrakes to help with landing
because Australian conditions were hot, with freaky
winds, and the aeroplane's gliding angle was too flat,
and he was critical of the DH86's directional stability.
But he agreed as time was running out to fly QEA's
first new machine on the long route to Australia, on
the vital delivery flight, if modifications could be made
later.

The take-off from Croydon on 24 September
was difficult because the DH86 was tail-heavy, loaded
to the maximum by de Havilland's with hardware for
the other side of the world—a spare engine in the
cabin, spare wheels and tyres in the back, spare
magnetos and other replaceable parts stuffed into all
the lockers. Brain flew down France and Italy, across
to the coast of Africa and along towards Egypt. That
particular morning the weather was perfect. The
Mediterranean away to the left looked blue and
beautiful. Lester Brain decided the time was appropri-
ate to go to the washroom at the very back of the
cabin. He had two crew lent by Imperial Airways, a
first officer already seated at the dual controls, and an

The de Havilland DH86 in flight
(Qantas Collection)

engineer, whom he now told to take the captain's seat
in the cockpit to keep weight up in the nose of the
tail-heavy aeroplane. When he was finished Brain
decided to try out the little jump seat positioned
outside the washroom. As he sat there alone at the
back of the cabin the plane yawed a little to the left,
then to the right. A few moments later it yawed more
severely to the left, and then to the right, then even
more severely, a heavy motion. Luggage fell out of the
hat racks. Brain clawed up the passageway as the
plane began to go into a flat spin. He pulled the
cockpit door open, ordered the terrified flight engineer
out of his seat and got the aircraft back under control.
They had lost three-quarters of their altitude. The first
officer was convinced that the controls had gone
wrong. It's a new aeroplane, thought Brain, so anything might happen. Their only chance of survival, he
reckoned, was to fly just above the calm sea and
within swimming distance of the shore, and they flew
on skimming the water until they reached the aerodrome at Mersa Matruh in Egypt. Brain switched off the
engines, turned off the petrol and made a dead-stick
landing. Nothing happened. Nothing collapsed. They
got out, immensely grateful to be alive, and checked
the aircraft's tail. Nothing felt loose, nothing was
broken.

Monsoon rain held them up in Calcutta. In
Burma they had to land on a submerged runway after
they had flown blind through wild lightning-filled
storms, and the gush of water along the aircraft's belly
ripped the fabric so it dangled down into the muddy
flood. The rain fell unceasingly for two days and
take-off was impossible. On the third day the sun
steamed out and the engineer patched the fuselage
with spare cloth and dope, and they flew on towards
Australia.

The DH86 was an attractive proposition to other airlines, and Ivan Holyman's new Australian National Airways, ANA, which planned services between Melbourne and Launceston in Tasmania, had ordered two of the single-pilot-control variety. The first was shipped out, assembled and began service on the first day of October 1934, weeks ahead of QEA. On Friday 19 October it disappeared at sea with the loss of the two pilots and the nine passengers.

The day after, Saturday 20 October, at 6.30 a.m. English time, what was described as "the most spectacular air race in the history of aviation" began. It seemed the ultimate test of the well-blazed England to Australia air route track—a speed race, with top pilots competing for a big money prize, and entries from all over the world. De Havilland's seemed to have an excellent chance of winning. Much of their energies over the last months had been devoted to the rushed designing and building of a small, sleek racing machine—the "Comet", the DH88. This was a prestige race, from Mildenhall (in Suffolk) to Melbourne, sponsored by the Australian chocolate millionaire Sir Macpherson Robertson to celebrate the centenary of the founding of Victoria. The Comet was built of the usual fabric and wood but it had two 225-horsepower engines and space for two pilots to alternate flying along the gruelling 18,000 kilometres (11,300 miles) in what would be an "all-out from the start" race.

Seventy aircraft were entered in the Centenary Air Race, and 20 started, among them three Comets. England—Australia veterans Amy Johnson and Jim Mollison, now married, were flying one black-painted Comet which flew non-stop to Baghdad then broke down in India. A Comet did win, painted red and piloted by another England—Australia route veteran and one-time Qantas pilot, Charles Scott, and Tom

Amy Johnson married record-breaking pilot Jim Mollison in 1932

Campbell Black, in an incredible time: one hour five minutes 42 seconds less than three days.

KLM had entered an aircraft flying the scheduled service to Batavia, extended for the purpose of the race to the finishing post at the racecourse in Melbourne. With what must have been exquisite pleasure, Albert Plesman announced that no particular concessions would be made for the race beyond the fitting of extra fuel tanks to his newly acquired DC-2. Three passengers would be carried, plus mail. After their long association with Fokker, KLM had rejected the latest version of a Fokker passenger aircraft when Plesman saw the American technological breakthrough. A revolution had begun in passenger aircraft and he had no intention of being left behind. The KLM DC-2 came in second, followed by a Boeing B247 leased from the American company Hudson Fysh had flown with, United Airlines.

The performance of the two American passenger aircraft stunned the public and confounded the British aviation experts, most of whom saw the American planes for the first time at Mildenhall. And why, it was demanded, will it take Imperial Airways and QEA 12 days plus to cover the same route? In vain did Hudson Fysh compare speed-cars with the family saloon, arbitrary one-off race conditions with the normal day-to-day functioning of a complex scheduled service, listing the time usually taken by KLM, pointing out the number of stops it would be necessary for the mail planes to make. The race tarnished the glamour of finally achieving a scheduled commercial service between England and Australia.

In the meantime QEA was frantically busy organising all the details of the new section from Singapore to Brisbane. So much had to be done. It was, after all, one-third of the total route. Qantas planned to cover the distance in three and a half days, which included the two longest dawn-to-dusk stages of the whole England—Australia journey. Accommodation had to be found where crews could spend the night, aerodromes chosen, agents appointed, food and drink organised, waiting places improved at airports, lavatories built, fuel and oil supplies set up by Shell, engineers appointed.

Imperial Airways planned to begin their first through airmail service from London on 8 December. Hudson Fysh remembered with passion standing at Fannie Bay, Port Darwin, on a landing ground he had chosen and built, watching Ross and Keith Smith fly in at the end of the first-ever England to Australia flight in December 1919. Now, 15 years later, he wanted to inaugurate the Australian end of the new route on the same day, 10 December. The Duke of Gloucester, who happened to be available, had agreed to open the service in Brisbane. It could be managed with just two DH86s, Fysh reckoned, until the other machines ordered by QEA arrived.

The second machine was being flown out from England heavily loaded like the first with spare parts. A young Imperial Airways pilot, John Lock, had been asked to fly it to Australia and he was thrilled. He had always wanted to get East and he had never been beyond Europe. At the last minute experienced skipper R. A. Prendergast, who had commanded *Astraea* the year before on her Australian jaunt, was needed urgently back in India. His home leave was cut short and he took the DH86 on its delivery flight instead.

Early on a fine clear morning, 15 November 1934, the DH86 took off with four engines roaring on the final day's journey, Longreach to Brisbane, for handing over at the QEA headquarters. Twenty minutes from Longreach it plunged into the ground

The wrecked DH86 near Longreach in Queensland, November 1934 (Qantas Collection)

with a sickening crash. Two kangaroo shooters making breakfast over their campfire ran to the wreck. The people from a nearby sheep station came, and police and a doctor and Qantas men out from Longreach. Four bodies were laid out by the crumpled wreck. In the afternoon Lester Brain flew up from Brisbane. He looked at the machine lying on the ground, the split, wrenched fabric, the broken tail, the fuselage pushed up into itself. He thought of the beautiful morning only weeks ago when he was flying towards Egypt, south of Tobruk, with the blue Mediterranean out the left window, and the DH86 beginning to yaw, and he thought, this could have been me. Had Captain Prendergast gone aft, just as he had, to the washroom at the back of the cabin, and put the engineer in the pilot's seat because the machine was so tail-heavy, and had he failed to get back in time to regain control as the aeroplane began its fatal spin? Brain found out from the doctor who was in which seat at the time of the crash. The first officer was in his usual co-pilot's seat in the cockpit, communicating with Longreach by radio. The engineer was in Captain Prendergast's seat in the cockpit. And Prendergast's body had been found in the rear of the cabin, just outside the washroom door.

Fysh was beleaguered. This was the second DH86 crash in Australia in four weeks, with no apparent cause. The public was jumpy and unnerved. Fifteen people were dead. The crashes were investigated and theories and explanations argued over. The new service could not be run with only one four-engined machine and now the Australian Director of Civil Aviation refused permission for the DH86 to be used on the Brisbane—Singapore route. The news, beginning to filter through that Imperial Airways was planning to scrap all existing aircraft types on the

Empire route and replace them with a new flying boat built by Short's as part of an airmail scheme, made Fysh's position even more difficult. He had to create faith in a machine which was now quite specifically a stop-gap. As a result of the Centenary Air Race everybody wanted more speed before the service had even opened. The as yet unbuilt Imperial Airways flying boats, being pushed as "safe over long sea crossings", would not apparently be much faster than anything the British had already: but they would be cheaper than the Douglas and Boeing aircraft and offer spacious comfort in the great British tradition of the sea, argued Imperial Airways. "We all want to go as fast as we can and waste the least time that we can, but ... speeds that are technically possible are not economically possible."

None of this helped Hudson Fysh, with a new service to get going in less than four weeks' time. Imperial Airways agreed to paper over the cracks by flying the whole route to Darwin, and handing over the airmail to QEA at the edge of Australia.

On Monday morning 10 December 1934 the Duke of Gloucester stood on a dais at Archerfield Aerodrome, Brisbane, and gave a smallish symbolic bag to Lester Brain. Brain heard him say, "I hand you this bag of mail to take to my brother the King," and received a limp handshake. It felt, said Brain, "like a cold fish". The bag contained the Duke's letters home to the royal family, and letters from the heads of Australian State governments to officials in England. "Captain Brain is kindly doing duty for us as Father Christmas," declared the Duke. "I have pleasure in declaring the Overseas Air Service open."

On the tarmac *Diana*, an old Qantas DH61, waited, newly painted and spruced up. The Duke cut a ribbon attached to one of its wings with a pair of

From left: Hudson Fysh, Lester Brain (pilot) and Mr H. H.
Harman, Secretary of QEA, before the departure of *Hippomenes*
on the inaugural flight of the Australia–England airmail service
on 10 December 1934
(Qantas Collection)

golden scissors shaped like propeller blades, the machine's single propeller whirred and the service was away. The weight of the 50-bag load of mail was shared by one of the old DH50s, *Hippomenes*. There was no payload spare for anything but mail because more had to be picked up on the route north. In Darwin on 13 December 55,967 items were loaded into Imperial Airways' four-engined Armstrong Whitworth XV *Arethusa*, and the mail reached England on 24 December. Father Christmas had only just made it.

In Croydon on the cold Saturday morning of 8 December 1934 the big HP42 *Hengist* was towed out of a shed by two caterpillar tractors and held in readiness while speeches were made, broadcast to the Empire by the BBC. A symbolic blue-silk mailbag containing letters from the royal family to Australia's Postmaster-General, and a special ivory and silver stamp which had franked them, were handed between officials. One hundred thousand pieces of mail and 227 kilograms (500 pounds) of parcels were piled up, waiting delivery along the Empire route. *Hengist* took off loaded with mail and passengers, and flying the new dark-blue and yellow Royal Airmail pennant. A second Handley Page followed to cope with the quantity of mail.

The Australian share of 66 bags, weighing 679 kilograms (1498 pounds), required two Qantas aeroplanes to carry it south from Darwin. The heated December air was full of turbulence, bucking the small machines, and a thick duststorm made flying very difficult near the Northern Territory border. The DH61 damaged her tail-skid taking off at Camooweal and a relief aircraft had to fly up and take over, but the airmail got through to Brisbane on 21 December. Included in the freight from England was a string-tied box of incubating hen's eggs, to be hatched in Sydney.

HP42 *Hengist* ready to begin the first England–Australia
scheduled airmail service on 8 December 1934
(Crown Copyright, courtesy of National Postal Museum, London)

Everyone heaved a sigh of relief to see the
service actually underway. "We got off to a scratch
and shaky start," said Hudson Fysh. Imperial Airways
was very stretched to run aeroplanes all the way
between Singapore and Darwin at such short notice.
The monsoons were beginning, from northern Australia up to Borneo. There was very little weather report-
ing, and only primitive radio. No passengers were
allowed officially to travel the route by the Australian
government until the service had proved itself,
although passengers continued to be carried inside
Australia along the old Qantas beat. The government
decision to locate the final terminus of the great route
at the inland railway station of Cootamundra was
causing much derision and anger. Brisbane got overseas news and mails flown all the way through by air.
The other southern cities had to wait for theirs while it
was off-loaded at Charleville and flown on south by
Butler Air Transport, to be taken onboard trains at
Cootamundra for distribution by rail.

The DH86 crisis continued. One flown out to
Australia by Imperial Airways was found on arrival at
Darwin to have a defective fin-post and bias gear. It
was immediately flown back to engineers at Singapore
who discovered that if the controls had been used to
check any major lateral movement, the fin-post unit
would probably have collapsed, causing a crash. A
fourth DH86 sent out by sea was found on examina-
tion in QEA's Brisbane workshops to have the fin-bias
transverse screw incorrectly located, a fault also found
on the machine wrecked at Longreach. Both of the
new machines had their Certificate of Airworthiness
suspended. The Australian members of the QEA board
were furious. The DH86 design, they were certain, had
been hurried and was inadequate. Cables shot back
and forth. On the other hand, the type was functioning

Postmaster-General Sir Kingsley Wood places a letter in the
mailbag for the first England—Australia airmail service (Crown
Copyright, courtesy of National Postal Museum, London)

in Europe without apparent problems. QEA engineers modified the fin assembly and made other adjustments to help with directional stability. "The DH86 trouble has had a disastrous effect on the initial life of the company such as is not possible to assess in cash value," reported Hudson Fysh to the QEA board in January 1935.

By February the civil aviation authorities were sufficiently satisfied to lift the ban on the DH86. At last Imperial Airways could be relieved of the route from Darwin through Singapore and it could become, as always intended, a QEA responsibility. An Australian airline would be operating internationally, with Australian crews—a moment of great joy for everyone connected with Qantas. The DH86s were prefixed with the initials RMA—Royal Mail Aeroplane—and named *Canberra*, *Sydney*, *Melbourne*, *Adelaide* and *Brisbane*. Lester Brain flew the opening service from Singapore on 25 February 1935, arriving in Darwin the next day. That same day the first outward mail left Darwin with Scotty Allan (now a QEA pilot) in command, and RMA *Canberra* made the Timor Sea crossing in three hours 10 minutes, although heavy rain penetrated the passenger cabin and flooded the floor.

The aim now was to function efficiently, get through the contractual trial period and qualify to run a passenger service. Fysh travelled the route inspecting what still needed doing. He had a horrible fright when the pilot of his DH86 touched down short at Seletar Aerodrome (the RAF base in Singapore) and managed to hop over a deep water-filled channel the width of a river. Fysh found the route still raw. Refuelling was carried out by hand at Brunette Downs using a chamois strainer as the Smiths would have done in 1919. He worried about lighting at landing grounds in case aircraft should come in late. Did local agents know how to use flares correctly? "Paint LADIES on Lavatory," he noted in his diary at Charleville. "Engineer should be in overalls," for Darwin. Accommodation was a problem in this frontier port, and QEA was renting a cottage on the cliff out by Vestey's meatworks. At least KLM were reputedly having difficulties settling the DC-2s into the Amsterdam–Batavia route. Tragically, the DC-2 *Uiver* that had flown so successfully in the Mildenhall–Melbourne race had crashed in December 1934 near Rutbah Wells, and investigations seemed to point to a lightning strike.

QEA's application to carry passengers was granted by the Director of Civil Aviation. A date was announced. Passengers could be booked to leave Australia by air from Wednesday 17 April 1935. Passengers would be able to fly from England all the way to Australia on the service leaving Croydon on Saturday 13 April. The longest commercial passenger service in the world was about to begin.

14

First Passenger Service

A SLENDER, DEEPLY TANNED 34-YEAR-OLD steps up into the cabin of RMA *Melbourne*. She is beautiful. She is the richest woman in England. She is racy and wilful, and her husband is King George V's cousin. She is becoming one of the most astonishing, spectacular and memorable women of the twentieth century. Airlines always long to lure the rich and prestigious as passengers; it is excellent for publicity and their image. Qantas Empire Airways is inaugurating its first overseas passenger service with one of the very richest, most newsworthy passengers possible, Lady Louis Mountbatten. Yet the publicity value is relatively muted. Edwina, Lady Mountbatten has been spending less and less time with her husband, friends and the social scene. She disappears for months at a time travelling the world on dangerous, taxing expeditions, usually with a woman companion. She is a restless and complicated person and travel seems to give her some release. This time her disappearance has been carefully veiled. She spent the end of 1934 in New York. "Edwina's black period", according to her friends, and no-one talks about it, although many speculate. Then, alone, she joined a sea-worn schooner at Tahiti and worked as crew while it travelled the islands, trading trinkets and beads for copra. No-one heard from her while she roughed it cleaning down the decks, standing watch, sharing the work with the rest of the crew. Qantas' publicity called it a "voyage in a schooner . . . cruising amongst tropical islands". Now, as always happens when she reappears, she has assumed the title and dignities of her rank.

Major H. Philips, Coldstream Guards, a friend of the Mountbattens, has booked as the first passenger on the first scheduled flight from Brisbane through to London, 20,526 kilometres (12,754 miles) of travelling. The wood and fabric biplane took off from Brisbane just after breakfast on Wednesday 17 April. This day's flying is rather tedious with a take-off and landing every 70 minutes, on average. The morning's stops are done—Toowoomba, then Roma for the traditional Australian morning tea and sandwiches, eaten in a hut at the side of the aerodrome while the aircraft is refuelled from a petrol pump. At Charleville lunch is served in town at a hotel, and Lady Mountbatten arrives with the mail from the south to join the flight. She wears a smart floral dress and attractive hat. Captain H. B. Hussey in regulation sun helmet, khaki shirt and shorts, hands her up the steps and into the narrow rectangular cabin which looks like a small bus, with five businesslike single seats down each side of a central aisle. The colour scheme is grey and dark green. There are nets above the windows for hats and light parcels, and broad window ledges for books and drinks. A veneered door leads straight into the control cabin—the "office", as Imperial Airways pilots like to call it, or the "bridge".

The vast State of Queensland, one-twelfth the

Lady Mountbatten, joining RMA *Melbourne* at Charleville,
Queensland, is greeted by Captain H. B. Hussey, 17 April 1935
(Qantas Collection)

distance to London, will be more than half-crossed this first day while passengers lounge back in chairs at 5000 feet, looking down on the rough ranges, the brown plains, the small settlements. "Who will make these seemingly lightning-like trips?" a journalist had asked. Australia to England by air means a complicated journey: 42 landings, five different aeroplanes, plus the French and Italian railways; nights spent in outback Australia, in the Dutch East Indies, in Siam (Thailand) and India, in the deserts of Arabia, in Iraq and northern Africa. "Arrivals and departures from all intermediate airports are approximate only," reads the timetable, "and services are liable to depart slightly ahead of time."

Edwina Mountbatten is an experienced air traveller. She always flies when she can. It saves time. The adventure of the first passenger service on the new route appeals to her. It can get her nearly to Malta, where Lord Louis is stationed with the navy, in a week and a half.

The night stop is at Longreach, two and a half hours short of the usual night's rest at the old Post Office Hotel, Cloncurry. Tomorrow will be a long day, eight take-offs and landings, nine and a half hours in the air. The call to wake comes before 5 a.m. A cup of tea and a biscuit, then the drive out to the aerodrome. In the cool earliness of pre-dawn the air is still and fresh. VH-USF is waiting. First Officer Sheppard takes delivery of the freight and mail, the luggage is stowed, the warning horn sounds, the engines start and the aircraft is away.

It is comfortable enough in the cabin. Leaving Longreach, this DH86 has spent a total of 264 hours 48 minutes in the air. The roar of the four engines has been deadened by special wadding packed between the

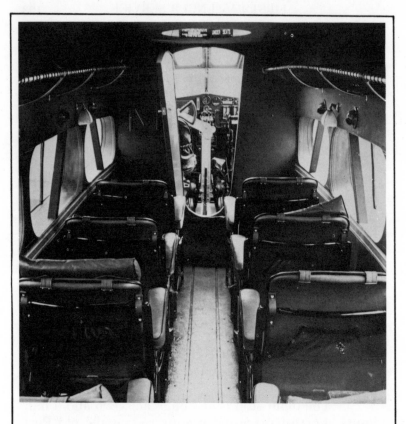

The passenger cabin, leading into the enclosed cockpit of the
DH86 (Qantas Collection)

linen skin of the aircraft and the inner wall, and cotton-wool has been handed out to stuff in passengers' ears. The chairs recline a little and there are adjustable foot rests. Individual air vents direct a flow of air and there really aren't any engine fumes, or smell of oil, to complain of. Barley sugar helps queasiness. The toilet room at the back of the cabin has a mirror and a washbasin with water from a tank.

There is a quick stop at Winton, then on to Cloncurry. The first officer has handed out drinks. Now he comes down the aisle to unlock the door, and Lady Louis and Major Philips climb out onto the red earth of the landing ground and stretch their legs. On, over lonely grey ranges, until the aircraft lands near the unexpected tall chimney and shafts of the mining town of Mount Isa for an exchange of mails, leaving behind a cloud of fine, penetrating dust at take-off. Camooweal for breakfast. The Queensland border, then the emptiness of the Northern Territory. Mail is dropped through a slot in the cabin door down to isolated stations. At Brunette Downs Aborigines stand watching while fuel is pumped into the aeroplane's tanks. Newcastle Waters, then Daly Waters for a late lunch and a quick cigarette before the final stage to Darwin, and the ocean.

The two days have been a kind of curtain-raiser, a prologue to the real adventure. Unavoidable, rather exhausting, but a revelation of the continent's vastness and the distances separating the remote clusters of people living along the route. And Darwin is a curious hybrid. Tropical with no graces. Tough but unsophisticated. Kindly but self-conscious. Neglected and friendly. It is Australia's front door, and it has not yet recovered from the shock of finding itself so.

Very early on Friday morning, 19 April, RMA *Melbourne* taxis into the far corner of Fannie Bay

Aerodrome and takes off out over the water. The first passengers on the first officially scheduled flight are being carried overseas.

In London the previous Saturday morning the first through passenger from England to Australia felt fidgety as he fingered his air ticket and walked around Airway Terminus, Victoria Station. The spring air made the buildings look dingy. In the streets the preparations for King George V and Queen Alexandra's Diamond Jubilee were already beginning. He would celebrate the Jubilee in Sydney, Australia, and he would get there having flown over the longest passenger air route in the world. But none of the other passengers waiting for the half-hour coach ride out to the airport at Croydon felt the excitement because this England–Australia air route began with an ordinary scheduled flight from London to Paris in a big HP42, and hundreds of people did that every month. And the tedious long train journey from Paris down to Brindisi on the edge of Italy, two nights and a day, as dirt from engine smoke crept onto all surfaces, was definitely not exciting. But Monday morning, before dawn, the train steamed around the curve of the harbour at Brindisi and the excitement began to run parallel with reality. All of the passengers in the Imperial Airways reserved coach were going part-way along the route— to the Gulf perhaps, or India. Only he, Richard Coke, actor and writer, was travelling the whole way. The ticket was not cheap: the price of a medium-sized car, or a year's wage if you were a draughtsman who had helped design one of these aircraft. It cost more than a first-class ticket on the England–Australia ocean liner, but the journey would be over in less than half the time.

Out in the harbour the big four-engined flying boat *Satyrus* waited, one of the three Short Kents built for the Mediterranean crossing. Bleary-eyed and un-fresh, the passengers ate early breakfast in a hotel. A motorboat took them from the quay out over the dark oily waters of the harbour to come alongside the Imperial Airways machine, riding head to wind at her moorings. A steward helped them aboard, checked passports, tickets and documents, and closed all hatches.

"All correct." The captain blows a whistle, the mooring ropes are released, and they are off on the real beginning of the Australian flight, the big bow wave curling past the hull and gradually flattening as the wings take the weight and the flying boat leaves the water, flies across to the island of Corfu, and on to Greece, with a mid-morning fuelling stop at Athens. Last month the Greek revolution made flying this way impossible, and schedules had to be altered. Travel-ling low over the Mediterranean with the windows partly open is pleasant. The crossing is punctuated by meals served on board: lunch as rugged Crete appears, tea as a narrow strip of white sand breaks the horizon ahead and the coast of Africa grows into the great port of Alexandria, bounded by desert dunes.

Satyrus arrives in Alexandria as travellers have always arrived—from the sea. It comes in past the lighthouse and the shipping to moor near three Short Calcuttas, the pioneers of the Mediterranean crossing, but now discarded. The joys of Alexandrian nightlife might call but a typed itinerary in the hotel bedroom reminds passengers of tomorrow's early departure. In the morning there is time for a cup of tea, looking out into the darkness of the harbour, before the phone rings announcing the long bus ride to the airport. *Hanno*, one of the 24-seater HP42s equipped for the long-haul imperial routes, is waiting, engines turning over, and within minutes the huge aircraft is away,

over the many mouths of the Nile, over desert and the
straight line of the Suez Canal, over more desert to
breakfast in a restaurant beside the small aerodrome
at Gaza, and the taste of grapefruit picked straight
from the tree. On over hard dry country, over the dark
unnatural stillness of the sunken Dead Sea, over the
desert with views of camels, two Arabs, one motor
lorry, nothing for an hour, then one car, to land at the
Imperial Airways fort and communications centre at
Rutbah Wells for lunch. Dawn this Tuesday morning
in the port of Alexandria, lunch at a fort guarded by
Arabs in the Syrian desert, 320 kilometres (200 miles)
from anywhere else, dusk in the ancient city of
Baghdad, flying much of the time along the desert
route: that first piece of the imperial airway hammered out by the pilots of the RAF at great cost and
individual courage, in the early 1920s.

Three hours' flying on Wednesday before landing for breakfast at the desolate airport and RAF base
at Basra at the head of the Persian Gulf, stopping
place of aircraft making for Australia since 1919,
beginning with the Smiths in their Vimy. Fuel is too
expensive in Iraqi Basra so an hour's flying brings a
fuelling stop at a mud-coloured town on the edge of
the Gulf, guarded by watchtowers and long walls like
a medieval painting, except that desert sand stretches
endlessly beyond. It is Kuwait, providing aviation fuel
from the lands of oil. An Arab thoroughly examines all
the aircraft's papers: "The trouble I cause you is
necessary for the protection of Kuwait and the Sheik,
my master." Three hours' more flying over the ex-
quisitely coloured shallow waters of the Gulf until a
cluster of islands is reached, with small towns, and
fishing nets positioned in great arcs. The Enchanted
Isles of Bahrain. The aerodrome is a hard sandy
stretch of ground behind one of the towns, with

The Imperial Airways sign at Gaza Airport, Palestine (RAF Museum, Hendon)

buildings of woven palm and matting. Thirty-five
minutes is allowed for lunch here at Bahrain, while
traders squat on the ground behind little mats display-
ing cheap pearls and carved pearlshell ornaments.
QEA might have Lady Mountbatten to grace their first
overseas passenger service, but Imperial Airways can
now boast an aristocratic passenger on a section of
their first passenger service to Australia. A young
Arab, brother of the Sheik of Sharjah, comes on board,
returning to his home from a pilgrimage to Mecca.

   Hanno flies away from the curve of the coast
and straight across the sea for three hours until, in the
fading light, the small city of Sharjah shows in the
desert beyond the shore, with the flatness of an
aerodrome backed by a large squat fort. A crowd waits
thisWednesday evening to greet, touch and embrace
the Sheik's young brother because he has returned
from Mecca. A procession moves to the Sheik's home
and welcoming Arabs fire their rifles up into the air.
The Imperial Airways passengers move towards the
safety of the fort, a hostile-looking building with
loopholes let into the battlements. Barbed-wire en-
tanglements close around aircraft and fort and a
bunch of the Sheik's well-armed guards stand sentry.
"They make Ali Baba's forty thieves look like choir
boys," comments a passenger. But they haven't much
to do and seem happy to barter bits of their equipment—daggers, belts, headgear. The Sheik has
guaranteed Imperial Airways immunity within a pre-
cisely defined three kilometre (two-mile) radius of the
fort. Notices read: "Passengers are earnestly requested
not to go outside the compound." But once inside
where well-furnished rooms lead off a central court,
where refrigerators and electric light and showers
make life almost luxurious, the Foreign-Legion surrounds fade away into the familiarity of home com-

forts. The fort is managed by the Imperial Airways station superintendent, a little wizened Englishman called Janes who has spent so long on the Gulf he is willing to live in this desolate place, hundreds of kilometres from the nearest European.

Grateful passengers can bathe because water is carried in from the nearest well in old petrol tins, heaped onto the backs of donkeys. Vast piles of petrol tins go in and out of the fort in procession. The Arabs use as many empty tins as they can get for every possible purpose. The aeroplane has brought a new carrying, cooking and building material to the desert.

Hanno's passengers are relaxing after dinner when the sand outside is suddenly lit by brilliant-white flares. The Handley Page is due in from India, and they rush out to stare up at the glow of cabin lights in the night sky, the huge expanse of wings edged by tiny specks of red and green light.

A 5 a.m. departure by moonlight on Thursday morning, breakfast served as the coast of Persia comes into view, and a landing at desolate Gwadar in Baluchistan after five hours in the air. Cups of tea are handed out in one of the rough shacks bordering the aerodrome while refuelling takes place. Here the second passenger of royal status boards the aircraft: His Highness the Sultan of Muscat, who occupies the forward cabin in dignified solitude while his entourage join the rest of the passengers in the rear cabin. "Do not give the royal party anything resembling ham sandwiches," the station superintendent warns the steward for the last time. After five hours of flying the landmark of Karachi is seen, the tall structure of the airship mooring mast, built for airships that never came. Here at the flat sandy aerodrome with its huts and hangars British and Indian officials are waiting to greet the Sultan and escort him to his car.

The Handley Page has ended its two and a half days of duty. A comfortable, majestically lumbering machine of sluggish speed, admirers call the HP42 the "flying hotel" and it does have a pantry and an icebox and steward service. Passengers continuing the journey from Karachi now join the smaller, rather less comfortable Armstrong Whitworth AW XV *Athena*, the same class as the *Astraea*, for a flight in a northward curve over dry brown-coloured India. As the daylight fades the air cools, the colours below turn mud-grey then blank out. Huge clouds loom and turbulent air forces the aircraft to judder and jolt. Lightning flashes across the sky. Just in time for some stomachs, the lights of a city show below and the aeroplane lands at the well-equipped airport at Jodhpur with its modern radio station, flood-lighting, control towers and administrative buildings, for Thursday night's stop.

There should be time to enjoy Jodhpur and there isn't. The ancient walled city on top of its hill, the Maharajah's excellent polo grounds, the beautiful gardens, the wearing of jodhpurs in their place of origin. There is hardly time to appreciate the luxurious hotel, built by the Maharajah next to the airport, with its servants, and furnishings of great taste and cost, and no time to swim in the large pool. Departure is before dawn on Friday along a flare-lit runway. There was elegance and comfort in Jodhpur despite extreme heat, and a sense of things missed. Breakfast is some hours later taken at the Delhi Flying Club, but there is only a glimpse of the fine city before departure again at 8.30 a.m.

India overwhelms the senses. There are two landings with mail and passenger transfers before the night stop in big humid Calcutta, and another dawn departure on Saturday morning. The aeroplane flies over the Ganges delta, thick dark mangrove swamps and twisting crocodile-infested rivers—the huge lonely ominous area of the Sundarbans, disliked intensely by pilots because there is nowhere to force-land. Swamps dissolve into a maze of islands, into mudbanks, and then the sea, and *Athena* flies on for an hour and a half over the Bay of Bengal before wheeling inland to come down at the little seaport of Akyab on the Burmese coast, with its pagodas and houses of teak. Breakfast is served in the upper room of a Burmese house, a short car journey from the airport.

With their load of mail and freight the Armstrong Whitworths only carry nine passengers and their range is poor, around 640 kilometres (400 miles). On this route there are heavy bookings for intermediate stages. A talkative Indian government official joins the plane at Akyab, and a Burmese gentleman, too, in a wide purple skirt, grey waistcoat and light-pink turban.

Coming into Rangoon just before midday the inner starboard engine exhaust pipe falls straight past the starboard windows down into a Burmese garden. A week ago the coach was leaving Victoria Station for Croydon Aerodrome. Now finding a new exhaust pipe in the Rangoon bazaar takes the rest of the day. The effects of passenger flying build up—not much sleep, unfamiliar food, constantly changing surrounds—and at this first week's end tiredness and numbness are setting in. Conversations have palled. The hold-up is welcome. It changes the pace, eases the routine of interrupted sleep, early starts and day-long flying. The night stay in Bangkok has to be jettisoned and the passengers tour the temples and the awe-inspiring, glittering, gold-covered, jewel-studded Shwe Dagon pagoda this steamy Saturday afternoon.

Take-off is delayed until 2.15 on Sunday morning. But sleep isn't possible. For the second time

Athena flies into violent storms, lightning splitting through apparently solid masses of cloud. The aircraft darts and jumps and falls and rights itself again through the turbulent air. Blind-flying, the captain tries to climb above the clouds, 8000 feet up, to 9000, 10,000, 11,000 feet. Chewing barley sugar helps, but paper bags are handed out. As so often, dawn is calm and delicately beautiful colours touch the clouds. The Armstrong Whitworths do not carry stewards, and refreshments are served by a young engineer returning to his post in Bangkok. Now he gets breakfast out of hampers—boiled eggs, chicken and rolls, with vacuum flasks of hot tea—and suddenly everyone feels better. The captain and first officer come back in turn to eat with the passengers. It is a night to remember but poor exchange for a night in Bangkok. The only time spent there now is a second very hurried breakfast at the airport while refuelling takes place and papers are examined by Siamese officials. The red tape along the route is endless. Every possible paper seems to need examining by at least one official. On, at 6.55 a.m., to make up lost time. But it is a day of sudden heavy rainstorms, waterfalls of water which leak into the cabin so it feels like a car with a poor-fitting hood. Alor Star for lunch and refuelling, wet as its reputation, then into Singapore after a furious deluge of cloud-black rain, all light withdrawn as the rain strikes viciously against the windowpanes and the captain flies blind. The landing is made at 5.50 in the evening at the RAF's Seletar Aerodrome, where hangars shelter the big bombers of Britain's eastern stronghold. The lost time has almost been made up, and Imperial Airways in partnership with Indian Transcontinental Airways hands over to Qantas Empire Airways.

It is more than pleasant to sleep at the world-famous Raffles Hotel. These great hotels at the cross-roads of travel are like clubs where friends meet unexpectedly. The final third of the journey begins at 5.45 a.m. on Monday 22 April. A week ago the big flying boat was taking off from Brindisi to cross the Mediterranean. Now a totally new section of route for scheduled passengers will be flown by Qantas Empire Airways in the recently and rapidly designed DH86. Experienced skipper Scotty Allan is in command of RMA *Adelaide*, four engines and a biplane like the huge HP42, but half the size, faster and with a greater range. The sun rises, ships lie gently at rest in the great harbour of Singapore, and the lights of the city slowly dim and are left behind as the aircraft heads south with six passengers. Seventy-five minutes after take-off there is a sudden lurch and Captain Allan opens the control cabin door and shouts "Equator!". Soon he comes out and suggests breakfast, served by the engineer, which is maybe not such a good idea because a huge four-course breakfast is waiting at the air-port restaurant in Batavia. So are Dutch officials in smart white uniforms, to salute the captain as he descends the stairs. From the restaurant KLM aircraft can be seen coming in to land. The grass covering the aerodrome is lush, vivid green tropical vegetation crowds the boundary. These landing places were just names in the stories of England–Australia record flights, now they are real.

The only night stop in the East Indies is gloriously different from the cosmopolitan Raffles Hotel of the night before, where a tin of cigarettes from the attentive waiter costs three to four times the price of the same thing in the street outside. Tonight on Lombok Island chickens scatter on the road to the rest house and several don't move fast enough as crew and passengers are driven past paddy fields, through

villages up to the cooler high ground. The rest house at
Selong is built of thatch and rushes with concrete
floors. Mount Rindjani rears its great height nearby,
clouds catching at the jungle-thick slopes. It is the
highest mountain in the Indies, 3691 metres (12,119
feet) of sharp-peaked extinct volcano.

The bath house needs to be explained to passengers. Built into the corner of the room is a tiled
concrete tank filled with cold water. Misunderstanding
the system and climbing in is a disaster. The prisoners
have to be fetched from the local gaol to empty the
tank and refill it. For correct bathing, water must be
scooped out with a special saucepan-like ladle as
needed, first to wet the body, then to rinse off the
soap; it is refreshing in the sticky heat. The lavatory is
self-explanatory: two holes in the ground with bottles
of water nearby.

After dinner there is time for a quiet smoke on
the wide verandah. The crew, as always, are hosts to
the passengers, chatting about the journey, answering
any queries. Their profession is someone else's adventure. The air ticket includes all accommodation and
meals and ground transport so there is little need for
passengers to concern themselves with different cur-
rencies. Only drinks have to be paid for, and tobacco,
and any personal stop-over activities. The evening is
warm. Then it is time for bed, two or three into each
large bed depending on numbers. Geckoes cling to the
bedroom walls with wide-spread toes, chirping endlessly. But everyone sleeps restfully under draped
mosquito nets like so many brides cocooned in white
veils. The time to get up comes soon enough.

Four a.m., Tuesday. Dress, tea and biscuits by
oil lamp, then the drive back to the aerodrome
through the darkness. The shadowy shapes of little
monkeys scuttle out of the headlights and around the

DH86 RMA *Adelaide*, flown by Captain Allan, refuelling at
Batavia Aerodrome, Java, in April 1935
(Qantas Collection)

aeroplane at the landing ground. Four hours of flying
over sea and islands, through rain and sun. Most of the
way from Singapore the DH86s have flown low
enough for passengers to see the detail of village roofs,
the texture of the sea, the structure of fish traps—to
almost sense the tigers in the dense jungle, the warm
wetness of paddy fields. It has been one of the most
exciting parts of the journey. Now the aeroplane comes
over Kupang, a little old port on the edge of the island
of Timor. The Dutch and the Portuguese fought a
battle here in 1653. In Timor the pioneer England-to-
Australia aviators waited for the dawn and gathered
their strength for the final journey, across the Timor
Sea. The aerodrome at Kupang is still only partially
cleared from the thick tropical forest, and it has one
windvane and a small tin building. An old Dutchman
with a stationmaster's flag salutes the captain then
escorts everyone across the landing ground to breakfast in the clean shed. Thick soup laced with bits of
sausage, fried onion and coconut; eggs and ham;
several puddings and coffee. The farewell meal in
Asia.

Allan flies the DH86 high above the Timor Sea,
9000 to 10,000 feet, out of boisterous winds at lower
levels. The sea is becoming the Qantas pilots' special
challenge—choosing an altitude by watching the
speed of cloud-shadows over the sea, and using the
information about wind direction gradually accumu-
lating at the meteorological office in Darwin. No
chance to see fish from this height, or giant turtles.
The passengers become drowsy, creeping along in a
light-blue sky with blue sea below, but the grey lining
to the cabin walls seems to cut down glare. They
glance at a magazine, gaze out of the window and wait
for Australia. The early risings and long hours in the
air have taken their toll.

Bathurst Island appears at 2 p.m. At 2.30 the white sand and red soil and grey-green timber of the mainland. At 3 p.m. on Tuesday 23 April the aircraft lands at Darwin. Customs officials get busy. The aircraft wheels have been sprayed in Kupang as a precaution against cattle disease, but the machine, only three to fours hours from Asia, seems a potent and potential carrier of many threats. The Australian authorities are using existing shipping regulations and adding new ones.

Darwin is not easy for the English traveller to immediately adjust to. Service and deference have marked the last 11 days. "There is much boisterous chatter in the hotel lounge, and at night a few 'drunks' propped up here and there along the main street, or being carefully shepherded home by handsome young policemen in attractive cowboy hats; picture all this ..."

A night is spent in Qantas' own bungalow, out by Vestey's meatworks and run by the redoubtable Mrs Ray. A pre-dawn take-off on Wednesday, sunrise over the bush, and breakfast in the corrugated-iron hangar at Daly Waters where mail is unloaded for Western Australia. Breakfasts over the past week have been in Iraq, India, Burma, the East Indies and now outback Australia, but this time shared with approximately a million flies. On again and some of the flies have hitched a ride in the cabin. They circle as irritatingly as ever, black buzzing tormentors while the aircraft bumps across loneliness, and lands at Brunette Downs, a cattle station where there is the excitement of a new passenger, a woman; then on to the mining town of Mount Isa. Outback Australia seems overwhelmingly huge and remote. Any landmarks to break the sameness appear about an hour apart. Late in the afternoon an aeroplane goes by, the QEA flight outward-bound from Brisbane to Singapore, the second to fly the new international passenger service out of Australia.

The last landing is made in the darkness along a flare path of oil rags blazing in tins, at Longreach, central Queensland. Nearly sixteen years ago two young air force officers, Hudson Fysh and Paul McGinness, came to Longreach to begin an overland survey for an air route through the outback for any pioneer airmen who might fly the enormous distance from London to Australia. Ross and Keith Smith's $27\frac{3}{4}$ days still look an incredible achievement. And now Longreach is an overnight stop on the England–Australia passenger route.

The man who has flown from London stares out into the bare, quiet streets of Longreach and thinks of his own first flight as a passenger, just after the Smiths' triumph—Le Bourget, Paris, to Cricklewood, London, in a converted Handley Page 0/400 bomber, sitting in heat and deafening noise in the bottom of the cockpit, with the legs of the pilot and his second-in-command dangling over his head. The novelty of 1920 has become commonplace: he has grown old in air travel.

Next morning there is the usual early departure, from a town which has seen airline passengers depart for almost as many unbroken years as any town on earth. Qantas began a scheduled air route here in 1922 and only KLM has been running a continuous airline service for longer. Once in the air the geography lesson of Australia is resumed as the DH86 works south and east, stopping, adding passengers, delivering freight, handing over the southern mail, until at last there is the sight of a river that opens onto a wide plain where there is a city, and beyond, the great Pacific Ocean. Brisbane, at 1.23 p.m., Thursday 25 April 1935. It is Anzac Day. The end of the Qantas

Empire Airways line, London to Brisbane in $12\frac{1}{2}$ days. The first passenger has landed.

In July 1935 Qantas was able to publish the kind of letter that warms the heart of an airline company. Lady Louis Mountbatten wished to express her appreciation:

"On arriving in Europe I am writing immediately to tell you what an extremely comfortable and interesting air trip I have had from Australia. I found both the Qantas and Imperial Airways' Services excellent and efficient in every way—and the personnel most courteous and obliging all the way through.

"It was a great and most enjoyable experience being on the first passenger-carrying service from Australia to Europe."

Appendix 1

SCHEDULED SERVICES: 1935 TO THE PRESENT

The first passengers flew on scheduled services between England and Australia in April 1935. The once-weekly service departed London eastbound on a Saturday, and Brisbane westbound on a Wednesday. (Arrival times are approximate.)

Saturday: 12.30—depart Croydon in an Imperial Airways' HP42 Heracles Class (38 passengers) for Paris.
17.15—depart Paris by train, changing at Milan for Brindisi, arriving 04.00 Monday morning.

Monday: 06.00—depart Brindisi in an Imperial Airways' Short S.17 Kent Class flying boat (16 passengers) for Athens, arriving Alexandria 16.30.

Tuesday: 04.45—depart Alexandria in an Imperial Airways' HP42 Hannibal Class with "colonial seating arrangements" (24 passengers) for Gaza and Rutbah Wells, arriving Baghdad 17.45.

Wednesday: 06.00—depart Baghdad for Basra,

	Kuwait, Bahrain, arriving Sharjah 19.30.
Thursday:	05.00—depart Sharjah for Gwadar and Karachi. Change to an AW XV Atalanta Class aircraft (nine passengers), Imperial Airways in partnership with Indian Transcontinental Airways, and on to Jodhpur, arriving 19.30.
Friday:	05.00—depart Jodhpur for Delhi, Cawnpore, Allahabad, arriving Calcutta 19.00.
Saturday:	05.00—depart Calcutta for Akyab and Rangoon, arriving Bangkok 17.00.
Sunday:	07.00—depart Bangkok for Alor Star and Singapore, arriving 18.00.
Monday:	06.00—depart Singapore in a Qantas Empire Airways' DH86 (10 passengers) for Batavia, Surabaya, Rambang on the island of Lombok, arriving 17.10.
Tuesday:	05.40—depart Rambang for Kupang on Timor, across the Timor Sea to Darwin, arriving 16.35.
Wednesday:	05.45—depart Darwin for Daly Waters, Newcastle Waters, Brunette Downs, Camooweal, Mt Isa, Cloncurry, Winton, arriving Longreach 18.30.
Thursday:	05.30—depart Longreach for Blackall, Charleville, Roma, Toowoomba, arriving Brisbane 12.30.

Westbound passengers departed from Brisbane at 08.00 on Wednesdays and arrived at Croydon at 12.05 on the following Monday week, $12\frac{1}{2}$ days later.

Timetables are never static. Adjustments began almost immediately: winter and summer schedules, withdrawal of several stops, local disturbances or wars causing route alterations. The frequency of flights increased, and the introduction of new aircraft brought about major timetable changes.

Journey time between England and Australia was cut to nine and a half days when the new Short C Class flying boats began operating along the whole route in the middle of 1938. Eighteen passengers could be carried, seated in comfortable cabins or relaxing on the promenade deck.

The war years, 1939 to 1945, disrupted the route between England and Australia. Vital mail, personnel and goods were flown on round-about routes. A Qantas-run Catalina flying-boat service across the Indian Ocean opened on 10 July 1943, with crews flying for 28 hours in the air, non-stop between Perth and Ceylon (Sri Lanka).

An express service taking 63 to 67 hours London–Sydney via the Indian Ocean began on 31 May 1945, using a civil version of the Lancaster bomber, the *Lancastrian*, with seats for nine passengers sitting sideways, and windows along one side of the aircraft only. The service included the world's longest regular commercial aviation stage, Singapore–Karachi, with a flying time of 13 to 16 hours. The crew of Captain, First Officer, Radio Officer, Navigation Officer and Flight Steward boarded fresh, and had several days' rest after completing the stage.

Hythe flying boats flew along the pre-war route via Singapore from 12 May 1946, taking a week. From Sydney, the Hythes stopped at Bowen, Darwin, Surabaya, Singapore, Rangoon, Calcutta, Karachi, Bahrain, Basra, Cairo, Augusta and Marseilles, terminating at Poole in Dorset. QEA and BOAC jointly ran both services.

Lockheed L.749 Constellations with pressurised air-conditioned cabins reduced the England–Australia route to four days at the end of 1947. QEA opened their first through service with the new American Lockheeds on 1 December 1947. Up to 38 passengers could be carried, sleeping at hotels in Singapore and Karachi, and spending the other two nights on the aircraft. They ate meals that had been processed by the latest quick-freeze techniques. The crew of Captain, First Officer, Second Officer, Navigating Officer, Radio Officer, Engineering Officer, Flight Engineer and three stewards included, from May 1948, an Air Hostess.

BOAC continued on the route with older aircraft types until they introduced Constellations on 1 December 1948. The last Hythe flying boat service arrived at Southampton from Sydney on 16 February 1949.

BOAC and Qantas introduced a once-weekly tourist-class service on the Kangaroo Route between Sydney and London in April 1954, reducing leg room and catering. "The tourist fare Sydney–London," claimed an advertisement, "is £298/15/0 (single) and £537/15/0 (return), approximately 20 per cent lower than first class ... All meals and night-stop hotel accommodation provided en route without additional cost." Regular first-class services continued to operate five times a week.

New Lockheed L.1049 Super Constellations bought by Qantas began flying the Kangaroo Route on 2 August 1954. Between 10 and 12 crew members managed 39 passengers on all-first-class flights, or 60 on all-tourist flights, or 27 deluxe-class and 30 tourist-class passengers on other flights.

On 2 March 1956, by eliminating the night stop at Singapore and overflying Jakarta and Bangkok, Qantas cut the Sydney–London journey time more than 20 hours to $54\frac{1}{2}$ hours westbound and 52 hours eastbound.

On 2 March 1957 BOAC introduced a new

London—Sydney service, flying three times a week with Bristol Britannia 102s, via Zurich, Istanbul, Karachi, Calcutta, Singapore and Jakarta, to Darwin. The first westbound flight left Sydney on 5 March.

On 3 May 1958 BOAC began operating Britannia 102 services between the United Kingdom and Melbourne.

At the end of 1959 jets were introduced on the Kangaroo Route. These cut into the journey time, reducing it to around 34 hours eastbound, and 37 hours westbound (because of prevailing headwinds). A Qantas Boeing 707-138 left Sydney for London on 27 October. The first eastbound 707 on the Kangaroo Route jet service left London on 29 October and travelled via Frankfurt, Rome, Cairo, Karachi, Calcutta, Bangkok, Singapore, Darwin and Brisbane, arriving in Sydney on 31 October.

BOAC began Comet 4 services from London to Sydney on 1 November 1959. By the middle of 1960 BOAC were running five Comet services a week with an average of eight stops, and Qantas had four services, using 707s and a chartered Comet, taking a slightly shorter time.

By mid-1962, using the new B707-138B, Qantas had an average eastbound flight time of 30 hours. A typical routing was via Rome, Istanbul, Teheran, Delhi, Bangkok, Singapore, Jakarta and Darwin, to Sydney. BOAC passengers could choose between a range of stops offered on its daily service, with a slightly longer flying time.

In 1963 the British introduced 707s, and by 1966 they had an all 707 fleet.

From November 1971 Qantas used Boeing 747-238Bs on the Kangaroo Route. In April 1972 British Airways added two 747s to the 707s flying the direct route. The big new 747 jets reduced travelling

time to around 25 hours eastbound and 27 westbound. Stops were cut from eight or nine to four to
five. Passengers could travel between England and
Australia via Hong Kong or the United States, as
well as by the direct route via the Middle East and
Singapore, and a number of airlines were now competing on the route.

By mid-1976 Qantas was offering a fastest
eastbound time, for London to Sydney via Bombay
and Perth, of 23 hours 25 minutes, and BA was
offering a fastest westbound service, via Singapore
and Bahrain, of 24 hours 15 minutes. In 1984 Qantas
offered a daily London–Sydney service via Bahrain
and Singapore of 24 hours 10 minutes eastbound and
24 hours 40 minutes westbound. BA offered a combination of stops and times, the fastest being via
Muscat and Singapore in 23 hours 20 minutes eastbound, and westbound in 24 hours 5 minutes.

Appendix 2

LOCATION OF HISTORIC AIRCRAFT

None of the Imperial Airways or Qantas Empire Airways passenger aircraft flying the England–Australia route before the beginning of World War II still exist. The B247 which came third in the 1934 Mildenhall to Melbourne race hangs in the Air and Space Museum in Washington, DC. The DH88 Comet which won the race is being restored to flying state and will be seen at air displays in the United Kingdom from the end of 1985.

Examples of World War I aircraft later converted to passenger use still stand in many of the world's museums. Qantas' first aircraft, the Avro 504K, has been reproduced and is stored at Sydney's Kingsford Smith Airport.

Some of the record-breaking aircraft which flew the England–Australia route have been preserved. The Smiths' Vickers Vimy is at Adelaide Airport. Bert Hinkler's Avro Avian is at the Queensland Museum, Brisbane (as is his Avro Baby). Kingsford Smith's *Southern Cross* is at the airport in Brisbane. Amy Johnson's Gipsy Moth *Jason* is in the Science Museum, London.

Index